Hockey

Zdeněk Pavliš

Hockey
First Steps for Kids

Meyer & Meyer Sport

Original Titel: Příručka Pro Trenéry Ledního Hokeje
I. Cást
© Zdeněk Pavliš, Tomáš Perič, 1998

British Library Cataloguing in Publication Data
A catalogue record for this book is available from the British Library

Zdeněk Pavliš:

Hockey
First Steps for Kids
Oxford: Meyer & Meyer Sport (UK) Ltd, 2004
ISBN 1-84126-152-1

All rights reserved, especially the right to copy and distribute as well as the translation rights.
No part of this work may be reproduced – including by photocopy, microfilm,
or any other means – processed, stored electronically, copied or distributed in any form
whatsoever without the written permission of the publisher.

© 2004 by Meyer & Meyer Sport (UK) Ltd.
Oxford, Aachen, Olsten (CH), Vienna, Quebec, New York,
Adelaide, Auckland, Johannesburg, Budapest
Member of the World
Sports Publishers' Association
Printed and bound: FINIDR, s. r. o., Český Těšín
E-mail: verlag@m-m-sports.com
www.m-m-sports.com

INDEX

Foreword 7

1   General Training Tips 9
Choosing Young Hockey Players 9
Teaching Principles 9
Dividing the Hockey Pitch up and Group Training 12
The Number of Assistants 15
Using the Time on the Ice to the Best 15
Close Quarter Playing 16
Using Aids 17

2   The Organization of Training 19
The Organization of Training Large Numbers (60) 19
The Organization of Training with 25 (30) Players 20

3   Managing the Training Process-Planning 21
Planning 21
The Training Unit 24
Methods and Forms of Organization in the Training Unit 28
Interactive Forms of Training 28
Methodical Tips for the Structure of the Training Unit 30
Training Controls and Recording Training Data 31
The Trainer's Training Diary 32
Player's Personal Data Card 33

4   The Role of the Trainer 35

5   The Parents 39

6   The Youngest Ice Hockey Player –
Main Aims of the Training 41

7   The Differences in Age and Development 43

8   Ice Hockey Methods 45

9 Methodical Tips for the Training of Ice Hockey Skills **51**
Framework Plan for 6 Year Olds 51
Framework Plan for 7 Year Olds 52
Framework Plan for 8 Year Olds 53
Example of a Four Month Ice-skating Course. 56

10 Individual Game Actions **57**
Breaking out Free with the Puck 62
Passing and Receiving a Pass 73
Shooting Techniques 81
Marking 91

11 Mini Hockey **99**

12 Training Examples for a Six Year Old **102**

13 Training Examples for a Seven Year Old **118**

14 Training Examples for an Eight Year Old **140**

15 Exercises **165**
Skating with the Puck and the Stick 165
Passing and Receiving a Pass 171
Shooting Training 176
Receiving the Puck 182

16 Appendices **191**
Symbols 191
Literature 192
Photo & Illustration Credits 192

FOREWORD

The successes of Czech Ice Hockey, in its 90-year history up to now, crowned in the second half of the 90s by winning the World Championships in 1996 and with the first gold medallion in Nagano in 1998, means that there is more interest being shown in the game from not only children, but also from parents and sponsors. Despite this positive change, compared to the beginning of the 90s, the number of active players in the Czech Republic is relatively small when put against those of the other world powers in ice hockey (Canada, USA, Sweden, Finland and Russia). This means that all the successes, which have been achieved to date and will be achieved hopefully in future, are due to the result of systematic work with players. For this the trainers of all age groups and performance standards are responsible.

In this book, besides introducing a certain number of exercises, theoretical knowledge and experiences, I would also like to go through examples from training that have been proved in actual practice by individual trainers. The main aim of this book is for it to be used as a methodical aid for the training work, principally with 6-8 year olds. Every trainer should work creatively with the book and develop the content according to his own actual requirements and personal philosophy. The book should also give the impulse for new ideas at the same time.

Zdeněk Pavliš

HOCKEY
FIRST STEPS FOR KIDS

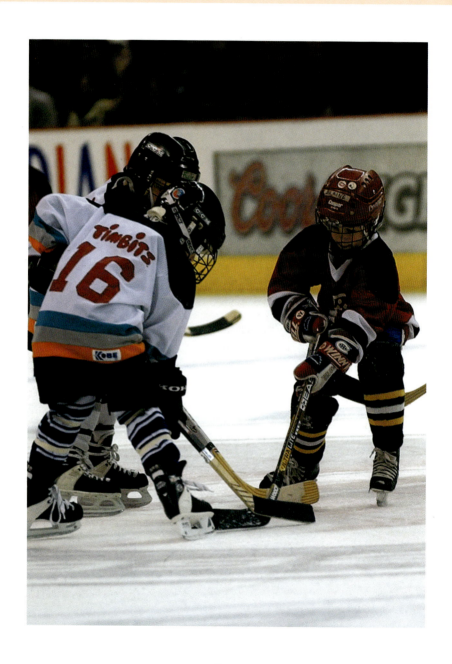

GENERAL TRAINING TIPS

Choosing Young Hockey Players

I t often tends to happen that children (at the age of 6 years old) are selected for a new team in an ice hockey club on account of their ice-skating abilities. This form of selection does not offer the best advantage, because instead of taking account of a larger number of abilities and skills, only one parameter is being considered. This method is partly acceptable if the lads have already taken part in a basic ice-skating course. Nevertheless, even in such cases, care must be taken in the selection process, because not all lads are at the same stage in their development (physically, psychologically and socially).

One question, often discussed, is how many lads in the 6-year old category should be selected. The answer is somewhat obvious – the more, the better. Experience has shown that the number of children, which one can effectively and efficiently still manage in the training unit, from both an aspect of space and organization, is about 60 children. Here, of course, we mean only one team. How many teams can be successfully trained by a club and play is very much up to the club itself.

Teaching Principles

The main sporting emphasis when training children must be to learn new skills and should not be to cover tactical training and stepping up the stress factor. It is very important to teach the children the new skills in the correct order. It is also important to know the methodical rules for learning the individual skills.

The development of the movement skills is called **motor learning**. This is a long process consisting of four phases. Basically the training of the individual phases is broken down into age and performance groups. There are the following phases of the motor learning:

- Generalization.
- Differentiation.
- Automation.
- Creativity.
- The sequence of teaching is characterized by didactical principles, which together build up a system that constitutes an effective teaching process. The most important didactical principles are:

1. The principles of education

Here it deals with the combination of training and education. In this connection, the following are important:

- To accept and value fellow team members, opponents and referees.
- Keep to the training schedules.
- To keep the changing-rooms clean etc.
- To be able to accept defeats.

The aim of the moral education is to guard against some of the negative tendencies such as selfishness or saying that the training is more important than school.

2. The principle of awareness and activity

This principle consists of the player;
- knowing what he will practice.
- having an idea of the solution to a task.
- knowing what the task is and what the aim of it is.

3. The principle of adequacy and appropriateness

The training process must adequately and appropriately match the physical and psychological development of the child. Nevertheless, on the other hand the challenge to the player must gradually increase in order to achieve further personal development.

4. The principle of clarity

A clear demonstration gives a way of explaining the content of a respective training session. The most effective ways of doing this are:

GENERAL TRAINING TIPS

- A demonstration directly on the ice (by the trainer or an active player).
- Video recordings.
- Pictures, illustrations.
- Each demonstration should be accompanied by a commentary.

5. The principle of systemization and taking things step by step

At the center of things is planning and the accomplishment of the plan. The plan consists of certain main points, which have to be mastered as a prerequisite for progress through the rest of the training process. In this book, therefore, there are recommendations for the methodical approach to training for each of the skills for each age group.

6. The principle of stabilization

The solidity of the skills gained is achieved by internalization, which here is called stabilization. Stabilization means either a positive or a negative assessment of the skill by the trainer. Positive assessment (praise) motivates the player and stability as well as self-confidence grows for future tasks.

7. The principle of individuality

The trainer should address the children as individuals as often as possible, above all particularly in the first few years of training. This, of course, sets the demand for sufficient numbers of assistants (either active players or parents).

The success of the trainer's work depends also on the selection of the training methods. The basic methods are especially:

- Demonstration.
- Observation.
- Explanation.
- Repetition.
- Passive movements (with the aid of a partner).
- Contrasts (right and wrong).
- Competition.

Some trainers sometimes use methods, such that the young players very often lose their own personal style and adopt the level of the average player in the team.

HOCKEY
FIRST STEPS FOR KIDS

This leads to the suppression of the player's personality. In the later training years, it is necessary to perfect the specific skills at the same time as the development of the ice hockey basic skills – for example, for a good shooter, shooting training has to be intensified etc.

Dividing the Hockey Pitch up and Group Training

The division of the playing field is very closely related to group training. Each group has its own section to itself in which they should stay and where they should practice their own training tasks. It is recommended that the playing sections be marked off using a band or cones. Sections of the same size can be arranged or other variations can be tried out. The smallest number of playing sections should be two and at the most six (see Diagram 1).

Diagram 1

GENERAL TRAINING TIPS

Dividing up the playing area for group training is also suitable off the ice e.g., in the sports hall or on a playground.

A basic requisite for the adequate division of the play area is having a sufficient number of children. Nevertheless, when 50-60 children are on the ice together, this calls for a particular organization of the training unit. The biggest problem, when training the youngest of the age categories, is the fact that not all the children have the same level of skills. It is, therefore, necessary to divide the children up into various groups according to performance criteria (e.g., the ice-skating skills). Up to six groups can train on the ice at one time, each group having 10 children. Each group works on its own without being hindered by another group. If a child in one group cannot keep up, it can be simply swapped over into another group where the pace of learning is slower. In this way, children with good talents for movement will not have "the brake applied" and vice-versa, those not so talented children will not be frustrated. The next diagram shows an example for dividing the team up into six groups.

One very important and often underestimated question is – where should the trainer stand? For this there is quite an obvious answer – that is, on the spot where he can see all the players, who are actively training.

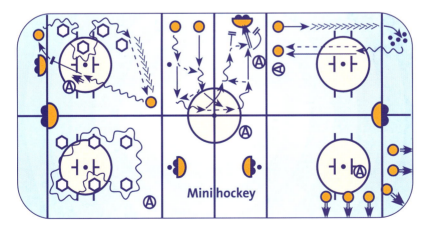

Diagram 2: Mini hockey

HOCKEY
FIRST STEPS FOR KIDS

GENERAL TRAINING TIPS

The Number of Assistants

The simultaneous training of between 50-60 children in the age group 5-7 years old, (initially one assumes that later on an average of about 10 lads will not take part in the training), requires a correction in the sequence of the activities of the players. We assume that in training 2-3 trainers are present and they devote the same amount of time to each child (e.g., one minute). This means that in the course of the 60-minute training unit, each receives personal contact 2-3 times. For technically difficult skills such as ice-skating this is too little. It is, therefore, important to have an adequate number of assistants available. Theoretically, it would be ideal if one grown-up was available for each child. In practice, this is understandably not possible. Nevertheless, a possible and achievable ratio is 8-10:1. In group training it is necessary to divide up a large group (50-60 children) into several small groups, with the assistants running the training. The main trainer does not have a group as he oversees the correct practice of the individual groups and leads the training of new skills. Active players or parents can be assistants, providing that they possess at least a certificate of competence as a trainer ('C' license). These basics are also valid for training with 25 (30) children. In that case at least 3-4 assistants are recommended.

Using the Time on the Ice to the Best

This is probably the most important principle in the training of children. The main aim of the sporting preparation in ice hockey is to master the necessary techniques that lead to later training. This consists of a large quantity of complicated skills so that the optimal and maximum use of the whole of the training time is tremendously important. The following recommendations give the best way to make a better use of the training time:

A balanced individualization of training and its control
(See Page 12 and Page 15 above)

The preparation of training
Warming up and stretching are best done off the ice so that only the actual training program takes place on the rink. The description of the exercises and the discussion over the content of the training should be done by the trainer in the

changing room so that no time is lost later on the ice. Then all the trainer has to do when on the ice is to name which training is to be done.

Carrying out relatively complicated exercises

This is about doing those exercises, which are always more demanding for the children with respect to their age and level of skill. An example of such things are doing a number of simultaneous passing movements, two or more shots at goal, doing a slalom round cones and so on. The background to this activity is that the children are required to carry out repetitive activities more than in a standard exercise, either at the same time or over a longer period of time.

Laying down pauses

For these periods, activities which are not so energetic and don't require much coordination are most suitable such as, for 2-3 minutes carrying out passing to a partner, then between three people, breaking out with the puck, shots against the side-boards, puck shots etc.

Close Quarter Playing

The way the pitch is divided up determines the amount that the players come into contact with each other. During a training session with 5 v. 5, using the whole surface of the ice, the lads often don't even get into possession of the puck during their time on the ice (about 1,5 minutes) and also spend a further 3-4 minutes on the bench. The time that the puck isn't in control of one of the players – either in a corner or on the other side of the playing area – is just as long. This example shows the disadvantages of using too large a playing area. We can achieve close quarter playing quite simply by dividing up the playing surface (for mini hockey it's most suitable to divide the area up into three sectors). When playing at close quarters, there is a lot of constant contact with the opposition. The children have to keep their eyes on the puck, teammates and opposition all the time. Because of this, two important training aspects are achieved; all the children – or at least most of them – get to play all the time and the skills are exercised intensively and repetitively.

Similar principles can be used when training off the ice. For example, variations of the classic games such as football, basketball, rugby, handball etc., which should

GENERAL TRAINING TIPS

be played on small pitches. A gymnasium can be divided up into three sections with football being played on one, basketball in another and rugby in the third one. Popular games such as catch can also be played in a small area better.

Using Aids

To achieve a high effectiveness in training, the aids that are suitable are those that, on the one hand, contribute to mastering the training content, and on the other hand, those that optimize the development of general movement skills. Here, we are talking about all kinds of equipment – cones, mini goalposts, obstacles, but also balls etc. Their use in the exercises (skating round, jumping over and skating underneath) plays an important role in the development later of the special skills. The number employed is also important. Each group in training must have a sufficient number to play with. Assuming that, for example, 15 cones are sufficient for older age categories, this means that when training six groups, each group has 2-3 cones. Nevertheless, a more suitable number would be about 5-8. It is similar when using balls. The number of balls suitable for training with children is one ball for every 2-3 children. That means a total of about 20 balls.

To increase the effectiveness of training, the skills should be also included and practiced off the ice. For this reason, technical exercises – stick work with small balls, shooting from the plate, simple machines (for shooting, skating etc.) A subject, often discussed, is the use of in-line skates. Opinions are varied, however, the kinetic similarity to ice-skating is extremely large. Also experience in ice speed skating argues in favor of a (limited) use of in-line skates in training.

A further, very useful aid that influences training effectiveness is the video technique.

HOCKEY
FIRST STEPS FOR KIDS

THE ORGANIZATION OF TRAINING

In practice, there are mainly two basic forms of organization. These are to do with the number of players, with either teams of 25 (30) players or teams with a larger number of players (about 60). These numbers appear to be the optimum ones for organizational purposes. If the numbers are higher, there is the possibility of dividing them up into two teams of the same size.

The Organization of Training Large Numbers (60)

In a club working with the highest number of children in the six year old category, the training of ice-skating skills (without a stick) is done first. Players are put into their age groups according to their birth date.

Because of the large number of players, training is organized into training theme stands. The necessary number of assistants is 5-6 per team and can be boosted by the help of parents or previous players as long as they possess a license of the lowest category. The main trainer is someone, to whom none of the children in the class belong, and who has a license of a higher category (or is in the process of gaining one). The license-system is different in the various national Hockey Federations, e. g. license A, B, C or I, II, III, IV, etc.

In the teams of the six and seven year olds, players seldom drop out because of a lack of performance. Where possible, one tries to push the talented ones on, who have begun ice hockey. The best lads from the youngest age group come up into the next age category (5-8 players). For this reason about 60 players with four goalkeepers take part in training.

Before the beginning of the new season, the first selection is made from the team with the eight year olds. The number of players is reduced to a total of 40 in two teams with four goalkeepers. The teams don't get to play properly yet. Only friendly matches are played so that the trainer doesn't come under pressure to achieve results. At the end of the season, another selection is made so that there are only about 33 players and three goalkeepers left, which are still divided into two teams.

The Organization of Training with 25 (30) Players

In a club working with 25-30 players in the six to eight year old category, the teams train in groups as well as using theme stands. If lads come into the team later, they are taken on and the training program is correspondingly reduced according to the skills mastered to date. Working together with the main trainer, there are, as a rule, 3-4 assistants, who have at least a license of the lowest category. As long as sufficient players remain in the category, the next selection is not carried out until they reach 10 years old.

MANAGING
THE TRAINING PROCESS

3 MANAGING THE TRAINING PROCESS-PLANNING

The complete training cycle and process cannot function (besides other things) without reliable and objective detail about what has to be included in training. In order to have an effective control system in training, certain conditions must be fulfilled – of importance are:

- Organization.
- Technical circumstances.
- Trainer.
- Economic considerations.

Personal training control contains four components, which are only effective when carried out at the same time and not individually. These are:

- Planning.
- Registration.
- Control.
- Evaluation.

Planning

We talk about **planning**, when it has to do with information pertaining to the future structure of the training. In other words – what will the content of future training look like?

One basic criterion for the planning of the sports program is the length of the session – the so-called training cycle. The length of each of the cycles is different, and sometimes is years or even only days. In ice hockey, both the training cycle, which lasts several years, as well as the shorter cycle are used. Every trainer has to know all the variations, in order to be able to put them into practice in training.

HOCKEY
FIRST STEPS FOR KIDS

The long term cycle

The plan for the long term cycle, sketching out the basic concept of the training, has to be short and concise. The aims for a period of 4-5 years are laid down. In practice, this cycle is used for national teams (the Olympic cycle) and above all for youths, where it comes into synchronization with the phases of the structure and building up of training.

Annual cycle

The year plan lays down a framework for the upcoming season in connection with the individual periods – so-called macro-cycles. Training for the technical, tactical, physical and psychological exercises are defined in these. The plan also contains an analysis of the problems and difficulties experienced during the preparation period in the previous year. In addition to team tasks, tasks for certain players are laid down. The general training parameters (the number of training periods, number of players (applicable to players from seven years old onward)) are all included in the plan. In ice hockey the annual cycle is divided up into four **macro-cycles**. These are the preparation period, the build-up period, the competition period and the transitional period.

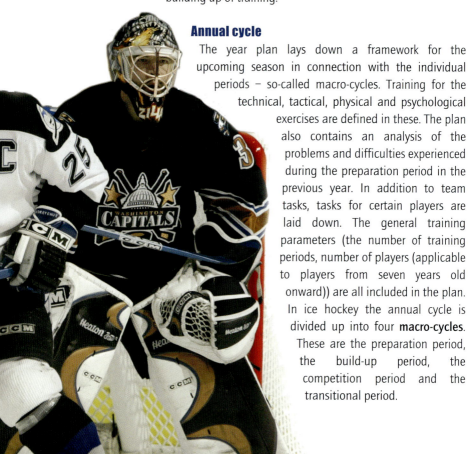

THE TRAINING PROCESS

Macro-cycles

The training plan for the macro-cycle describes the individual periods in phases of several months. For this time, the content of the training and the use of training aids are laid down in detail for each period. In this way, the plan constitutes an important form of aid for the trainer.

The preparation period – this lasts from the middle of April to the end of June. Training sessions do not take place on the ice. For the 6-8 year olds, 2-3 periods per week are recommended.

The build-up period – this begins in August/September with training on the ice and ends with the first match. For the youngest age group, this period carries on over into the competition period. For all age groups, preparatory exercises on the ice are mixed together with exercises on firm ground.

The competition period – or alternatively called the **main period**. This is made up mainly of two or three sections. This period lasts from September until the end of March.

The transitional period – this begins at the end of the season and lasts up until the beginning of the training for the preparation period. For the youngest age category this period contains no special training aims.

Meso-cycle

This means a mid-term cycle that lasts 2-4 weeks. Several individual meso-cycles form the macro-cycle mentioned already. In practice, various different variants of meso-cycles are used. However, these concern mainly the older playing cadres.

Micro-cycle

This is a short-term cycle of between 2-10 days. It consists of several training period units. For youth teams, the term weekly plan is often used. In this part of the plan, the content and aims of the individual training periods are listed.

HOCKEY
FIRST STEPS FOR KIDS

The Training Unit

The training unit is the basic measure of time (i.e., unit) in a cycle. It derives its content from the micro-cycle (for 6-8 year olds from the weekly plan) and concretely covers the training requirements. At the same time, the training unit is the basic unit of organization in the training process. Using them, the long-term aims are achieved, i.e., the content of each training unit should be built up on top of each other.

The length of a training unit ranges between 45 minutes up to several hours (2-3), of which the latter, however, should only be for the older age categories in the preparatory phase in the hall. For the 6-8 year old category, the length of the training unit should be 60 minutes on the ice and otherwise no more than 90 minutes.

A training unit is basically divided up into 3 or 4 phases:
1) **Beginning**
    a) Warm-up.
    b) Preparation.
2) **Main part.**
3) **Conclusion (cool down).**

The first part of the training unit is seen as the preparation of the organism and the mental attitude of the player for the exertion and the main part of the training.

Psychological preparation
■ The player must be told about the aims of the training unit; he should understand what is expected of him in the upcoming challenges and be prepared to concentrate at the right moment.

Preparation of the body and respiratory organs as well as the cardiovascular system
■ The initial exercises concentrate on stretching and warming up the muscles, sinews and joints. The intensity of the exercises increases gradually so that a reaction is reached in the system's functions.

24

THE TRAINING PROCESS

Preparation for the activities that follow in the main part

Beginning

The whole of the warm-up is varied. In our case, it takes up to 10-30% of the time of the whole training unit (10-20 minutes). The beginning can have two variations:

a) General part – consists mainly of deliberate exercises.
b) Special part – the organism is prepared for the exercises in the upcoming main part.

In practice, a further division of the beginning phase is used:

Warming up – lasts about 10% of the whole time (5-7 minutes). The main aim consists of explaining the content of the whole training unit and in warming up the body. The training unit should always begin by greeting the children.

Preparation – this takes about 10-20% of the whole time (5-15 minutes) and is orientated towards the main part of the unit. The warm-up, stretching and freeing up of the muscles is achieved by doing exercises, which are closely related to the content of the main part of the training.

The main part

The total time for this training section normally ranges between 50-70% of the training unit (25-45 minutes) and usually contains the following exercises (or a combination of them):

- Training of and perfection of the technical and tactical skills.
- Development and internalization of the individual skills in movement (speed, power skating, agility, stamina and fluency). Deliberately targeted development of the movement skills is, however, not done until the later age groups.
- Internalization of the structure of the sporting performance – this is where higher performance levels are being striven for.

A permanent element of the main part of training, in the period for young players, is the **game** itself. For the category of the 6-8 year olds, the game is played on a small surface (mini hockey), or alternatively different variations of little games on the ice can be preferred.

HOCKEY
FIRST STEPS FOR KIDS

In practice, the training exercises have the following logical sequence:
1) Training of and perfection of the technical and tactical skills.
2) Exercises for the promotion of coordination.
3) Training of speed and power skating skills.
4) Strength training.
5) Stamina training.

THE TRAINING PROCESS

The arrangement of the plan only gives a rough overview of the exercises and is mainly, above all, designed for the older age groups. Care must be taken that the build-up of the exercises in the training period matches the aim of the training. As an example, for the main part of training in the 6-8 year old category, the training of skills can be designated as the aim.

Any new skill should be demonstrated and practiced at the beginning of the training period straight away after the warm-up. It is important that the players should not be too tired (both physically and mentally) when doing the exercises.

When practicing skills that are already familiar in training, these exercises can be done in the second half of the main part of training. The build-up of the training period for players in the higher performance level is quite different from that to be employed in the beginner group levels.

Conclusion (cool down)

The conclusion (or cool down) of the training session must ensure a smooth transition from the strain of the training to the gradual calming down of the organism. The correct structure of this section has an influence on and accelerates the recovery process that follows on.

The cooling down process lasts between 7-10 minutes. This is about 10% of the total time of the training session unit. The content of the cool down depends on the characteristics of the exercise strain in the main part. The main aim is to moderate the functions of the body system and the winding down of the mental processes. This is done by doing less intensive exercises (skating slowly, jogging etc). In the second half of the cool down, do stretching exercises. Above all, stretch those muscle areas that have been put particularly under strain during the training.

For all age groups, the training period should finish off finally with a joint debrief. In this the trainer goes over what has happened in the period and outlines the next training session.

HOCKEY
FIRST STEPS FOR KIDS

Methods and Forms of Organization in the Training Unit

The training method, as well as its organizational form is determined by external circumstances. The intervention of an opponent and the degree of being able to adapt to the game situation mark these circumstances. In practice, three forms are used.

Preparatory exercises – these are exercises without an opponent, for example, a player dribbles with the puck and at a particular spot (the face-off spot) he shoots at goal.

Game exercises – these are characterized by the intervention of the opponent, for example in a 1:1 situation.

Game situations – these are characterized by the presence of an opponent and a certain amount of coincidence. This takes the form of a freely developing game, but with rules. With roles continually changing, moving from attack over into defense and vice-versa is an important factor here. There are several possibilities for game situations – as follows:

- Setting special rules.
- Setting up little games where the content is more along the lines of the rules in ice hockey.
- Setting up the game situation deliberately.

Interactive Forms of Training

Interactive forms of training relate to the activity between trainer and the players during the training as well as the interactivity between the individual players themselves. In practice, the differentiation is as follows:

- Joint forms.
- Group forms.
- Individual forms.

Joint forms

The whole team does the exercise under the direction of the trainer. This exercise form demands a lot of organization and control. This form should not be used too much with youth teams, above all, because the various abilities and skills of the individual players cannot be assessed and controlled sufficiently.

THE TRAINING PROCESS

Group forms
The team is divided up into several, small groups. They are grouped together taking note of the following factors:
- Performance ability (according to the ability of mastering the skills – above all, ice-skating).
- Specialization (defender, attacking forward).
- Organizational unit (two defenders, three attacking forwards, all five players). Each group has its own task. It can have various forms.
- All groups have the same task that they accomplish either with the same form or with another form (e.g., all groups practice ice-skating, whereby, nevertheless, the differences in performance or various tasks of the individual player are taken into account).
- Each group has a different task and these are done at theme stations. After a predetermined time the group moves on to the next station and changes tasks.

Individual forms
Each player practices at his own pace and develops his ability individually. In this case the training is adapted to the individual. This training form is very suited for the development of the player's independence and his creative thinking.

HOCKEY
FIRST STEPS FOR KIDS

Methodical Tips for the Structure of the Training Unit

- During the competition period, the training period should take place 2-3 times a week on the ice. In addition to this, it is recommended that, once a week, training should be held in the gymnasium. The length of the training unit on the ice should be 60-75 minutes.
- Each training period includes a game (mainly held on a small pitch – mini-hockey).
- Training should be structured so that the predominant part of the exercises can be done in the form of a proper game. For children, exercises lacking an emotional touch, are very uninteresting and they soon get bored. When they play, they are capable of working for long periods without tiring. Many exercises can be structured as game forms, and if this is not possible (for example, when practicing skills) it is important to alternate training activities with game forms (catching games etc).
- Once the basic skills have been partially mastered, you should practice attack and defense maneuvers equally. In practice, this means: skating forwards and backwards, passing, taking the puck on and tackling.
- Work individually with children as much as possible.
- Start off each training period by creating a good, suitable atmosphere.
- Similarly, also end each training period by collecting everyone together. A little praise will result in the children looking forward to the next training session.
- Because of the possible loss of concentration, the length of each of the exercises should be no more than 5-7 minutes. The trainer should react immediately to any changes in concentration and either shorten the exercise or change it altogether.
- For the 6-8 year olds, specialization on any of the playing positions should not yet be undertaken, and thus positions should be constantly changed around. One exception to this is the goalkeeper.
- It has proven to be advantageous when the club puts on ice-skating courses for all those interested (irrespective whether they carry on later or not). This allows the trainers to put more lads into the six year old teams, or to put in more talented players in the seven year old and exceptionally the eight year old team. The skating course lasts usually 3-6 months under the direction of

THE TRAINING PROCESS

one of the experienced trainers (sometimes also under the direction of the figure skating trainer), and takes place without using the ice hockey stick. This practice is common also in other ice hockey playing countries like Russia, Canada and Finland.

Training Controls and Recording Training Data

By the term control, here we mean the comparison of the training aims set and the actual achievement of those aims.

Recording training data relies on continually capturing and recording what the content of the training was and an assessment of all of the player's characteristics (performance ability, evaluation of the training parameters etc). Correctly recorded training data give the trainer creative work in training methods to be used.

Training data records principally concern recording:
1) The organization of training, the training content, the quality of the training and the teamwork in the team leadership.
2) The performance ability and the attitude of the whole team as well as individual players;
   a) in training.
   b) in competition.
3) The qualifications and personal data of the player.

The performance ability or the individual effort can, basically, be either judged subjectively – the trainer assesses the player from his own viewpoint and from his own experience – or it is judged by using objective parameters.

Within a club, in practice, it is usual to record the number of goals scored, the number of successful passes that led to scoring a goal (+/-), the number of minutes spent in the sin bin, the effectiveness of outplaying the opposition and the goalkeeper's activities etc. By using the objective parameters, one can differentiate separately between the play of two defenders, three attacking forwards or between all five players. The trainer himself must decide which type of parameter he will use.

HOCKEY
FIRST STEPS FOR KIDS

Besides the assessment of the ice hockey player's training performance of the ice hockey player, other parameters, which have an influence on the performance ability, can be called upon. This means measuring the physiological functions, such as somatic type, in order to be able to assess the movement abilities – this is done by using various motor tests etc.

Generally, training data is sub-divided into the following groups:

General Training Data:
- Number of training days.
- Number of training session units.
- Number of training hours.
- Number of matches played.
- Number of recovery and regeneration hours.

Special Training Data:
- Strain load content of the training.
- Intensity of the training.
- Type of strain load.

The capture of training data for the older age and higher performance categories is typically the same.

The Trainer's Training Diary

The trainer's training diary is an essential part of training planning and the capture of data in ice hockey. The trainer's training diary should contain:
- The game plan.
- Player participation in the training.
- The framework plan for the work-up to the competition match.
- Plans for the individual preparatory periods.
- Plans for the individual training session units.
- Preparation, analysis and evaluation of the competition match.
- Continuous assessment of the player (objective and subjective assessments).

THE TRAINING PROCESS

Player's Personal Data Card

Every trainer should keep precise and comprehensive notes on the personal data and specialization of each player. Usually these take the form of a card for each person. These cards can then be handed on to the trainer's colleagues when the player moves up into a higher age group. Ideally, the card should be started when the player begins at the age of six and follows him up into the senior categories.

The player's personal data card should contain the following:

- Personal details (name, address, birth date, telephone number and parent's contact details).
- Particular data (how the stick is held, positions played, objective training parameters, motor test results, strengths and weaknesses, general health and educational aspects and examinations etc.)

HOCKEY
FIRST STEPS FOR KIDS

TRAINER'S ROLE

THE ROLE OF THE TRAINER

It is difficult to describe the role of the trainer because he carries out a specific leadership activity. Despite all the difficulties, we are going to try to list the main demands that a trainer has to deal with in his work with the youngest age groups.

For lads, who are beginning ice hockey, the trainer represents an important personality. His qualifications, training and skills influence the newly won experiences of the young players as they start out to learn about ice hockey, or any sport for that matter, for the first time. How well he will get on mainly lies in the hands of the trainer. His role is therefore very important. The lads can only gather positive ice hockey experiences, if the trainer is able to put them over in a suitable and adequate manner. A trainer, working with the youngest age groups, plays a decisive role in the process of motivation. It depends on him whether the new sporting experiences will or will not motivate the young players.

The trainer influences the young players in every way – physically, mentally and socially. Every role that the trainer takes on demands a great deal of responsibility, because he represents an example – a role model – to his charges. The young players often copy everything that they see or hear by saying, "The trainer said so", or, "The trainer does it that way."

When we speak of the trainer's role, we think of him as teacher, tutor, leader, organizer etc. For these various different roles let us list the principles that are typical for a certain role. However, one must never try to lock each of them into a firm categorization. They constantly change around.

The following aspects make up the most important ones in the trainer's job:

- The content of the training (which the player's have to achieve in each of the age groups) must be firmly in the trainer's mind.
- He has to use the correct methods when teaching and perfecting the skills, because not all ice hockey skills (e.g., skating, puck handling) are easy to

35

learn. Some of them continue to be practiced in all age groups. This is why you shouldn't give up practicing those skills, which are only perfected when you reach the older age groups.
- Group training, where the players, who for the moment are not learning so quickly, are also allowed enough time to practice.
- When working with the youngest age group, an appropriate form of language should be used.

TRAINER'S ROLE

- Training should also contain more than just the passing on of the skills of ice hockey; the lads should also learn other skills (physical, mental and social ones), which will serve them also in normal life.
- After training, the trainer should give feedback to the lads and their parents. The trainer must be able to listen to "feelings, opinions and ideas" and this is an essential additional task in his work.
- To be able to find the best spot, in order to direct the player's training activities and the assistant's work to the best.
- To plan the time and space aspects of the training effectively.
- The trainer's manner should always give an example to the lads; honor and truthfulness are important characteristics.
- To have a good rapport with children. The children should be positively motivated. They need an agreeable atmosphere, be able to have fun playing and not just be pressurized to have to participate in the training. The lads should be encouraged and praised. Generally, the proportion of praise (positive assessment) and criticism (negative assessment) should be about 3(or 4) : 1. When criticism is necessary, it is better to begin with the positive aspects, and then to draw attention to the mistakes; for example, "The passing was rapid and exact, but too late – the player wasn't unmarked anymore". In all assessments, general figures of speech should be avoided (e.g., "That was poor – the pass was rubbish").
- As an authority, the trainer should take an interest in the school marks of his charges. In any case, he should not ignore poor school marks or conspicuous behavior in the classroom. If there are punishments meted out, they should not be allowed to influence training motivation to any great degree.
- The players should respect the opposing players, the referees and officials.
- The personality of each individual player should be developed harmoniously with an acceptance of the difference in age, while at the same time taking consideration of the personal perspectives.
- The trainer should plan the player's activities, lead them, organize them and control them by employing an individual 'approach' to each player.

Very important is the continuation training of the trainer himself, because well educated trainers work more successfully and with more competence and will be valued by the players more.

HOCKEY
FIRST STEPS FOR KIDS

ROLE OF THE PARENTS

THE PARENTS

I n the first few years of training, the parental influence is large because of two reasons; on the one hand, children at this age need a certain amount of help when putting on their kit or getting to the rink. On the other hand, the engagement of the parents is important for the sports club when thinking about sponsors. This can be in the form of either, just supporting one's own child, or in the role of a sponsor, who more or less helps the team or club financially or materially.

- For these and also other reasons, the parents get involved in the training process. They make judgements about the training and influence what is happening in the team. It is very much up to the trainer, how he uses the positive inputs and minimizes the negative influences.
- In order to keep the negative influences down to a minimum, the trainer should explain to the parents:
  - What role the trainer and his assistants have in the team.
  - The aims of ice hockey, the training and yearly program.
  - The responsibility of the parents and their influence on the smooth functioning of the team.

The most effective way to achieve a good working relationship with the parents is to hold discussions with them regularly. Holding a meeting in the course of the season appears to be a very useful way of doing this. It is recommended that such a meeting should take place prior to the first joint training session. Using this opportunity, the main content of the training can be explained to the parents:

- The role of the trainer and his assistants.
- The program for the whole of the season together with the main working aims.
- The danger of injury and preventative measures (suitable equipment and where best to buy this).
- Player obligations – the punctuality for training and a game, possession of the mandatory equipment for training and a match, keeping to the training times

HOCKEY
FIRST STEPS FOR KIDS

– with the exception of overriding grounds – sufficient sleep, normal basic hygienic habits (tidiness and cleanliness in the locker room etc). All these things should be discussed with the parents, so that they will make sure that their children comply.

■ The responsibility of the parents, who help in deciding whether their child is fit and can take part in training. Parents also help to explain what terms such as *winning* or *losing* etc., mean. The parents should understand and know the principles of the ice hockey rules – this helps both the trainer and the children themselves. The parents are responsible for the children's behavior on the ice and for them participating in training and matches etc. The parents (especially ones who have played themselves) should be advised that they can be involved in the team as an assistant trainer, providing that they hold at least a 'C' license.

Thus the role of the parent in the training process can be very useful and helpful. On the other hand, parents can also be a negative influence. It is important for the trainer to find the right relationship with the parents, so that they take on the responsibility and become active with the team. Despite this, it is equally important that the trainer keeps a little distance between himself and the parents. In no way should they get involved in the training process, team training and match business.

MAIN AIMS OF TRAINING

THE YOUNGEST ICE HOCKEY PLAYER – MAIN AIMS OF THE TRAINING

The sports training for the youngest age category should provide the children with good entertainment, fun and pleasure at moving about. No way should the atmosphere be spoiled by stress about competition. It is not a typical way of training, like those sessions that follow in later years and above all as a grown-up. The main emphasis of the activity is maintained in playing games and learning the basic skills.

This includes:
- Ice-skating.
- Getting past a player keeping the puck.
- Passing and receiving a pass.
- Shooting.
- Tackling the puck off someone.
- Close quarter play.

Main aims of training
- To give joy and pleasure in playing ice hockey.
- To provide an atmosphere suitable for maintaining fitness, for partaking in entertainment and for learning.
- To develop communication and individual interaction between the children.
- To learn to accept the opposing player and develop the sense of fair play.
- To allow the player to have fun playing and to learn the new skills playfully.
- To develop the important basic skills for ice hockey (speed, coordination, balance, power, courage etc).

Training in these categories can be defined as follows:

The character of training – introduction of the elementary technical ice hockey basics, and the establishment of a friendly atmosphere.

HOCKEY
FIRST STEPS FOR KIDS

Training attitude – create positive conditions for the balanced development of a player's personality, preparation for further phases in sport.

Training content – the basics of the technical and tactical skills are taught in specialized lessons while technical and tactical situations are conveyed in a playful form.

THE DIFFERENCES IN AGE AND DEVELOPMENT

In ice hockey, systematic training activity starts first of all in the sixth to seventh year. From an educational point of view, this age is **exactly the right age to start**. At this age, children are easily lead and their interest in their environment and also in sport is continually growing. Their physical development is characterized by regular growth of their organs and their weight and height gradually increases. Their organism also becomes more resistant. Their skeletal frames have not yet completely developed, so it is not yet recommended that the spinal cord and the larger joints (hips, knees, and shoulders) are placed under stress. It is important to concentrate on a good, correct posture, because ice hockey can lead to damage to a good one.

The motor system (aspects of movement) in a child depends on the function of the central nerve system, bone development and hardness, and from the development of the muscles inter alia. At the beginning of this period in life, the lads should be able to master the basic movements and basic sporting activities such as skiing, swimming and cycling. This period in life can be broken down further into the age groups:

- 6-7 year olds – this age group is marked by restlessness; the children are unsteady, always on the move and show an increased urge for activity.
- 8-10 year olds – this period in life is known as the "golden age for the motor system". The reason for this is that children of this age can learn movement skills the easiest – it simply requires a correct demonstration of what is required.

Psychological development is predicated on the training of the child's personality. It is marked by impulsiveness and unsteadiness. The child can only concentrate on an activity for no more than 5-7 minutes. Longer intensity (for example explaining a game variation) is not possible. Changes in the child's social environment have a very strong influence on it. Above all these include starting at school, training in a team and the development of making friends. The child begins to have more sensitive feelings and characteristics – fairness, courage, and sticking to its word.

HOCKEY
FIRST STEPS FOR KIDS

METHODS
TRAINING BUILD-UP

8

ICE HOCKEY METHODS

Even before the framework plan is laid, which contains all the individual skills that the players in their different age categories have to learn, the complete method of playing hockey should be explained. A complete overview of the game's activities gives the possibility of extending particular aspects of the training program. This is first of all possible when the players can master the relevant skills quickly.

Ice hockey is a game where the players try to score as many goals as possible. In ice hockey there is a difference of two phases – the attack and the defense.

On the attack, the team in possession of the puck begins actively to either threaten the goalie and get a goal or to keep hold of the puck.

In defense, the team without the puck tries to get possession of it, in order to avoid a goal being scored against them or to start their own attack. These two phases contain the so-called **game play activities**. From the viewpoint of the method, they are divided up as follows:

1. From the aspect of the team's activity with the puck:
■ Attack actions.
■ Defense actions.

2. According to the number of players, taking part in the action:
■ Individual game play actions.
■ Game play combinations.
■ Game plan.

When speaking of the term **ice hockey method**, we mean a basic overview, the differences as well as an explanation of the game itself, in which the individual players (individual game play actions), or groups (game play combinations), or the whole team (game plan), take(s) part.

45

HOCKEY
FIRST STEPS FOR KIDS

Ice-skating

Ice-skating is a basic skill and should be dealt with separately. Ice-skating consists of the following individual skills:

1) **Skating forwards.**
2) **Skating backwards.**
3) **Trick skating.**
   - Change of speed – braking and stopping.
   - Change of direction – skating a curve and doing the cross-over.
   - Turns.
   - Starts.
   - Other skating skills.

Individual game play actions

This means the complex movements that a player uses to help carry out or overcome different game situations. From a theoretical, sports educational viewpoint, and from actual practice (training and competition), the actions are separated out into attack and defense actions.

Individual attack actions

1) **Breaking away free with the puck by:**
   - Taking the puck on forwards.
   - Taking evasive action.
   - Other variations – doing a turn, changing direction, changing speed, passing with the skate etc.

2) **Breaking away free without the puck by:**
   - Changing direction (doing a cross-over, skating in a curve, doing a turn).
   - Changing speed.

3) **Giving a pass and receiving a pass**
   - Giving a pass:
     - Forehand, backhand.
     - Flat on the ice – over the ice without contacting the surface.
     - Direct pass – off the boards.
     - Wrist flick shot – full shot.

TRAINING BUILD-UP

- Receiving a pass:
  - Forehand.
  - Backhand.
  - Receiving an inaccurate pass.

4) Shooting techniques
- Forehand:
  - Wrist flick shot.
  - Short snap push shot.
  - Full push shot.
  - Golf action shot.
- Backhand:
  - Wrist flick shot.
  - Full push shot.
- Penalty shooting.
- Deflection shot (tip-in).
- Follow on shot.

5) Faking and dummies
- With the body.
- By changing direction.
- Faking with the stick.

Individual defensive actions
1) Marking the player in possession of the puck by:
- Attacking (the opponent).
- Tackling the puck away.
- Tackling the man.
- Body-checking.

2) Marking the player not in possession of the puck:
- In the open.
- Close up.
- In a position between the opponent and your own goal.
- In a position between the opponent in possession of the puck and an opponent without the puck.

3) Area defense:
- Marking an area.
- Marking a player in a particular area.

4) Blocking shots at goal:
- In a standing position.
- On one knee and on both knees.
- Using a swinging glide.
- With the stick.

Game play combinations

This concerns variations usable by two or more players working together, either on the attack or in defense in different game play situations.

Attacking combinations
1) "Passing and evading being marked".
2) Crossing.
3) Back or 'drop' pass to be taken on by someone else.
4) Forming a shield.
5) Starting off in a free unmarked area.

Defensive combinations
1) Doubling up.
2) Protecting.
3) Taking on.
4) Handing over.
5) Marking the man.

The game plan

The term **game plan** means the conscious playing of a situation (on the attack or in the defense) by using the cooperation of the players in a team. The effectiveness of the result depends not only on the technical and tactical skills used as well as the fitness and physical level of the individual players, but also, above all, on their understanding of the game and the business of working together.

TRAINING BUILD-UP

Game plan in the attack

1) Continual attack.
2) Positional attack.
3) Rapid attack.
4) Quick counter-attack.
5) A re-organized attack.
6) Puck shot in the attacking zone.
7) Positional play concentrating on the attack zone.
8) Outnumbering the opposition.

Game plan in defense

1) Zonal defense.
2) Marking the man.
3) Combined defense.
4) Applying pressure in zones.

Specifics

These include
- The face-off.
- The goalie's actions.

The goalie's tasks

1) **On-guard position.**
- Skating in the goal area.
- Positioning in front of the goal.
- Positioning behind the goal and skating around it.

2) **Catching, stopping and hitting the puck out.**
- Flat shots over the ice using:
  - The legs.
  - The stick.
  - The body (sideways gliding swing).
- Puck shots over the ice at half height using:
  - The hands.
  - The legs.
  - The stick.
  - The body (sideways gliding swing).

High puck shots using:
- The hands.
- The body.

3) Stick play
- Stopping the puck.
- Playing the puck out.
- Kicking the puck out.

4) Penalty shots
- Moving out from the goal mouth.
- Kicking the puck out.
- Doing a knee split (on one knee or both).
- Sideways gliding swing.
- Catching the puck in the air.

5) Game play situations
- By covering the shooting angle.
- Saving a concealed shot.
- Saving a shot on the rebound.
- When a dummy shot is made.
- When play comes in from behind the goal mouth.
- In a 2:1 situation.

METHODICAL TIPS

METHODICAL TIPS FOR THE TRAINING OF ICE HOCKEY SKILLS

Framework Plan for 6 Year Olds

The training of technical and tactical skills should take place in a logical sequence, and so we offer the trainer a framework plan (methodical tips) for each of the age categories. Individual skills serve to act as a control, where their perfection is a requirement for the training to go on. The first plan is for lads, who haven't done a basic course in ice-skating.

Ice-skating
- Standing upright.
- Maintaining the balance when standing.
- Moving on the ice.
- Keeping the balance when moving.
- Changing skate blade edge.
- Doing a curve – doing an inside and an outside curve.
- Gliding for a distance.
- Skating fast round a curve.
- Sideways movements.
- Forward cross-over of the skating leg.
- Stopping using a one-sided snowplough.
- Simple trick skating (slalom, jumping over or ducking under obstacles).

Other activities
- Little games.
- Game variations on the ice.
- The basics of dribbling with the puck (for players, who have already mastered ice-skating).
- The basics of passing (for players, who have already mastered ice-skating).

HOCKEY
FIRST STEPS FOR KIDS

Framework Plan for 7 Year Olds

Ice-skating
- Keeping the balance when standing and on the move.
- Skating on the blade edge and changing edges.
- Gliding for a distance – the 'T' position is emphasized.
- Skating forwards in small tight curves.
- Doing the forward cross-over – practicing the push off from either leg.
- Stopping – the one-sided plough.
- Doing a half curve when skating backwards.
- Doing the cross-over backwards – rhythm.
- Stopping when skating backwards doing a one-sided plough.
- Basics of the start – stepping forwards with rapid high frequency steps.
- Turns – doing a 'three-step turn'.
- Stopping, using the swinging stop on either side.
- Stopping when skating backwards.
- Turns when skating backwards – the three-step – basics.
- Turns when skating forwards – the three-step – basics.
- Turns when skating curves forwards and backwards.
- Trick skating – slalom, ducking under and jumping over obstacles and various variations of these.

Dribbling the puck and other player activities
- Short and longer dribbling when standing still.
- Short and longer dribbling when on the move.
- Dribbling with the puck in a curve.
- The basics of evading actions.
- Passing play and control of the puck when standing still and when on the move (forehand and backhand).
- The basics of shooting – the short, slap or pull shot – the puck lifts up.
- Dribbling the puck through a simple slalom – skating forwards.

Other activities
- Little games.
- Game variations on the ice (football, handball, rugby etc).
- Mini hockey.
- The rules – basics (the offside rule, the icing rule (illegal clearance)).

METHODICAL TIPS

Framework Plan for 8 Year Olds

Ice-skating - continued improvement of ice-skating skills already learned

- Cross-over backwards - used when skating backwards.
- Doing short, tight curves with stops.
- Rhythmical cross-over forwards.
- Stopping when skating backwards - all variations.
- Turning to skate backwards when skating forwards and vice versa (the three-turn aka the three-step)
- Starts in a forwards and sideways direction after stopping when skating backwards.
- Doing a full turn using the cross-over when skating either forwards or backwards.
- Practicing ice-skating skills on a slalom course and other trick courses.
- Basic maneuvers.
- Accelerating while doing medium and wide curves.
- Developing ice-skating skills with the right technique at high speed.

Dribbling the puck

- Dribbling the puck with short actions and long actions skating forwards and in curves.
- Dribbling the puck skating forwards or backwards on a slalom course with tricks: jumping over and ducking under obstacles (puck control).
- Dribbling the puck skating backwards and in curves with speed-ups.

Breaking out free with the puck

- Evading maneuvers - forehand and backhand, wide evading maneuver on one side.
- The basics of faking.
- Dribbling the puck when skating backwards.
- Covering the puck using the body.
- Basics in a situation 1:1.

Breaking out free without the puck

- Practicing being continuously on the move and passing in a free area.

HOCKEY
FIRST STEPS FOR KIDS

Passes and puck control
- Doing passes and controlling the puck in different situations (frontal, sideways).
- Passing with emphasis on accuracy.
- Passing when skating backward.
- Seeking out unmarked areas to be able to receive a pass (player breaking out free without the puck).

Practicing shots on goal
- Lifting the puck when shooting from a standing position and on the move.
- The short, slap or pulled shot (forehand and backhand).
- Exploiting all the various shooting possibilities.
- Controlling the puck when applying pressure in front of the goal and making use of the rebound.
- When in a potential shooting position, keeping the stick down on the ice.

Marking the player in possession of the puck
- When marking, the player should utilize all the various skills.
- The basics of tackling the puck off someone with all its variations.

Working together
- The basic positioning of the players (3-2; three forwards and two defenders).
- The basics of movement in the game area (each player has his own area).
- Playing into the unmarked areas (moving and passing).
- Game variations on the ice (using the various basics already mentioned for working together).
- Mini hockey.
- Knowing the basic rules (offside, icing, two-line pass, body-charge or body-check penalty)

METHODICAL TIPS

HOCKEY
FIRST STEPS FOR KIDS

Example of a Four Month Ice-skating Course

Lessons 1-6

1) First of all, attention is paid to:
- The basic ice-skating position.
- Moving on the ice (the correct use of the skates).
- Maintaining the balance and paying attention to the correct position of the body weight.
- Learning to push off correctly from the inside edge of the skate (practicing from the rink edge rail first of all and then doing it on the ice without support).
- Skating forwards on both skates combined with balancing exercises, knee bends, and changes of the center of balance of the body.

Lessons 7-16

2) Training concentrates on:
- Practicing and revising skills already learned.
- Perfecting skating forwards and doing the start and glide correctly.
- Skating in wide curves on both skates.
- Being able to do the cross-over with both legs skating forwards.
- Stopping using the one-sided plough (practice both legs).

Lessons 17-31

3) Training concentrates particularly on:
- Practicing and revising skills already learned.
- Stopping using the swing stop on both skates (left and right swings).
- Skating backwards.
- Practicing the turn into a backwards skating motion from the forwards skating posture.
- The basics of doing the cross-over when skating backwards.

Lessons 32-35

4) While these lessons are being carried out, the skills are tested and the selection of the lads (approx 60 players) takes place for the next season's team. The players selected carry on with the training in the March. The parents pay for the cost of the training (preparation of the rink ice).

10
INDIVIDUAL GAME ACTIONS

Individual play in a game is made up of actions, which consist of attacking duties by the individual player (in the team in possession of the puck at the time) and of defensive duties of the individual player (in the team not in possession of the puck). These actions by the players in the two teams make the play mutually conditional. The aim is to hold the puck in a zone or to wrest it from the opponents, in order to, in so doing, push in an attack or to prevent one being carried out against your own goal. In the 6-8 year old age group a lighter weight puck is recommended, in order to optimize the training of individual skills. Following on with a methodical approach, training of the ice hockey skills in the form of the following activities is recommended:

Individual attack actions
- The player being able to break out free with the puck.
- Passing and receiving passes.
- Shooting a goal.

Individual defense actions
- Tackling the puck off an opponent.

Before going into the correct technique for the individual skills (individual game actions), it is necessary to list a few basic factors:
- The optimal length of the hockey stick.
- Holding the stick correctly.
- Quality of the stick and the correct binding on the blade end of the stick.

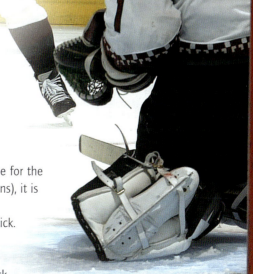

57

The optimal length of the hockey stick

For youngsters playing, the correct length of the stick is an essential prerequisite for effective puck work. The length can be measured as follows:

- Without skates on, the stick should reach up to the nose when standing upright.
- With skates on it should reach up as far as the chin (see Diagram 3).

Diagram 3

The trainer should insist on each age group having the correct sized stick. Parents often argue against this, saying that because of the rate of growth the child should have a longer stick, which itself is not advantageous anyway.

When dribbling, if the elbow of the upper arm holding the stick is not able to come round in front of the body, then the stick is too long. Besides this, the size and length of the blade end also plays a role. Young players, should in no way use a stick with a long, broad, blade with too curved an end. When choosing a stick,

GAME PLAY

the angle between the shaft and the blade end is often ignored. You should always choose a stick with which you are able to adopt the correct basic position.

Later, with older players, the choice of stick depends not only on body height, but also on the player's strength and ice-skating skill. At the top end of the shaft is a knob, which prevents the stick slipping out of the upper hand. As a result, the knob has to match the size of the child's hand in order to ensure that the stick is comfortable to use. Rubber knobs are not suitable for the youngest players. They are too large for this age group and this leads to the stick being held incorrectly below the knob.

Holding the ice hockey stick

Dribbling the puck well depends on holding the stick correctly. Young players hold the stick always in two hands, with one hand at the tip of the shaft (known as the "upper hand") and the other hand nearer to the blade end of the stick (known as the "lower hand"). The hands are held apart at about shoulder width (see Diagram 4).

Diagram 4

Dependent on the position of the lower hand on the stick we speak of a **left-handed grip** (with the left hand underneath) or a **right-handed grip** (with the right hand underneath). The trainer must make sure that the stick is held correctly, especially with beginners. An aid to making sure of this is to use initially a broom handle, for example.

The upper hand grasps the stick by the knob, held in the palm of the hand. The grip is quite firm and the stick is moved around using the wrist. The lower hand holds the stick in the area where the fingers join the palm of the hand (see Diagram 5). Here the grip is held alternately loose (for example when receiving the puck) and firm (when shooting at goal). Also, this hand can be slipped up and down the shaft (dependent on activity – taking evading action, doing a golf shot etc).

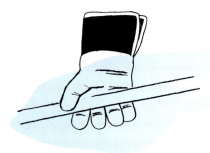

Diagram 5

Stick quality and binding

A further aspect, which influences play with the puck considerably, is the quality of the stick as well as its elastic binding. It's mainly the parents, who now and again come out with the misconception that the level of skill has nothing to do with the quality of the stick ("......a good player can play with the branch of a tree"). But the reality is totally the opposite. The quality of the stick considerably influences the level of skill. This is why the trainer should take care that the players use good sticks (particularly where it concerns the blade area). Damage in this area should be avoided.

GAME PLAY

The same applies to the binding, which plays an important role in ice hockey. Above all, the blade should be bound, in order to ensure better puck handling in all the skills. The binding must, however, not present an obstacle. This often happens when the binding is applied in several layers (a new layer over an old layer). Binding in the area where the shaft turns into the blade is superfluous – puck handling is not improved this way. 'Sandwiches' of bindings has the disadvantage of adding weight. For this reason, it is worth removing the old layer, let the stick dry out and then to apply the fresh binding. Ideally, the binding should be started 2 cm from the toe of the blade, and end off 2 cm away from the point that it turns into the shaft (see Diagram 6).

Diagram 6

Breaking out Free with the Puck

Breaking out free with the puck is one of the attacking actions in ice hockey, by which the player gains a better position for further game play (passing, trying to shoot a goal). By getting round behind the opponent you achieve an outnumbering situation for your own team, increase the effectiveness of the attack and create the necessary conditions for a successful outcome.

There are three basic variations of breaking free:
1) Puck handling
- Dribbling.
- Stroking.
- Pushing.
- Dribbling the puck closely or further out.

2) Taking evading action.

3) Other forms (by turning, kicking the puck with the skate etc).

The technical prerequisites for all variations of breaking out with the puck include:
- Adopting the basic position for a player with the puck and the appropriate grip on the stick.
- Peripheral puck control.
- Continuous contact with the puck by the blade.
- Faking a shot by using the body (aka a body deke) and the blade of the stick (aka a stick deke).
- With the puck.
- Covering the puck using the body.
- Watching the defending opponent (and his stick).
- Accelerating after an evading maneuver.

The technique and tactics used in breaking out with the puck are influenced by the following inter alia:
- The game situation.
- The game area.
- The opponent's defensive actions.

GAME PLAY

The basic position when breaking out with the puck

The player grips the stick with arms out in front of the body at shoulder width. Where required that the puck should be dribbled in any direction, the shoulders and the elbows must be held relaxed. The knees are slightly bent (similar to the basic position when ice-skating) and the torso and the head are held upright. The eyes are watching an area of the game 5-7 m around the player (see Diagram 7).

Diagram 7

Peripheral puck control

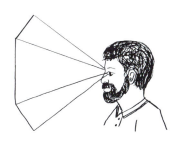

Diagram 8

This term means keeping an eye on the puck without constantly having to look fixedly at it. When dribbling the puck it should be kept between the middle of the blade and the area where the blade moves up into the shaft. The head is held upright so that the player can observe where his teammates and the opposition is, and so that, at the same time, he can keep control of the puck with his stick. Having wide peripheral vision is essential for the ice hockey player. The player is aware of the puck at all times, but can also concentrate at the same time on the situation on the ice. Tunnel vision, where the player is constantly looking only at the puck, is a typical mistake made by beginners; such players have not yet developed sufficient feeling for the situation. They have to keep their eyes constantly on the puck so that it doesn't jump away from the stick. With peripheral puck control, the player watches the game play and keeps an eye on the puck with the lower part of his visual perception (see Diagram 8).

Puck handling

Puck handling is one of the basic skills when breaking out with the puck. The player tries to gain a better position to start or complete an attack.

The player can move the puck by:
- Dribbling.
- Dribbling the puck closely or further out.
- Stroking.
- Pushing.

Dribbling

Dribbling is the most used version of puck handling. The puck moves in front of the player's body and approximately in the middle of the blade. In dribbling, the blade of the stick is held at a constant angle towards the puck (see Diagram 9). The movement stems from the wrist. It is important that the fingers and not the thumb hold the stick and that the shoulders and arms are kept loose.

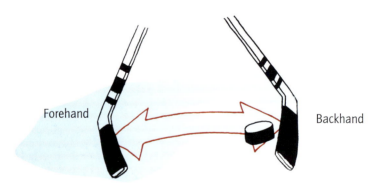

Diagram 9

Dependent on the radius of the movement of the stick you do either a tight close dribble (the movement is kept at shoulder width) or a wide dribble. Important here is the way the lower hand glides up and down the shaft of the stick and the actions of the wrist movement (see Diagram 10).

GAME PLAY

The player controls the puck using his peripheral vision and stick feeling. If the player only watches the puck when dribbling, he loses sight of the opponents and the positions of his own teammates. Young players have to practice this skill time and time again so that they develop a 'feeling for the puck' and so that they can change rhythm when dribbling.

Diagram 10

Dribbling the puck closely or further out

This manner of puck handling is used when the player is facing an opponent, or when he is about to do a fake or make a shot or a pass. This version is used not only by forwards but also defenders.

The puck is moved parallel to the body (not to the skates) on the forehand (see Diagram 11). Here it is important to use the correct wrist movements and to hold the blade of the stick at an angle towards the puck. You are looking forward so that the puck remains in peripheral visibility.

Diagram 11

Puck handling by stroking

This version is used mainly when skating in a curve or when doing a cross-over. It is also used when skating round an opponent carrying out a long evading movement, or when attacking by using the boards with a change of direction afterwards.

Principally there are two possibilities:
- Stroking on the forehand (see Diagram 12).
- Stroking on the backhand (see Diagram 13).

The puck is lead on diagonally to the side of the player. The player grips the stick mainly only in one hand and with the other (inner) hand he blocks the opponent. The inside shoulder and the leg that is projected forward slightly when skating in a curve, is used to protect the puck prior to poking it out, and before striking it. When doing this it is important to keep the puck as far as possible forward away from the body.

When stroking on the forehand, the upper arm blocks the opponent. On the backhand, the stick is gripped in the upper hand and the lower hand blocks the opponent. The blade of the stick is angled steeply against the puck. Holding the body too upright and leading the puck on too closely, as well as having the blade at an insufficient angle to the puck, are all mistakes.

Diagram 12

GAME PLAY

Diagram 13

Puck handling by pushing

Diagram 14

This version, where the puck is hardly protected, is used when one is making a quick start to get into a free area. The stick is gripped in the (upper) hand with the arm held bent loosely ready to move the puck on. The stick blade is angled towards the ice and the puck is pushed forwards in front of the body (see Diagram 14). Evading maneuvers with the stick held in one hand is tiring and is used regularly, first of all, by older players. The lower hand is left off the stick and is used to assist in accelerating.

Generally, a common mistake with young players lies in them having too much of a right angle between the blade and the ice. This causes the puck not to be far enough away from the body. At the same time, it is wrong to hold the stick right at its end (stick handling is strenuous and the puck cannot be lead optimally).

Methodical tips for correct puck handling

- Dribbling close while standing still.
- Dribbling close while moving forward slowly.
- Dribbling wide while standing still and on the move.
- Changeover between close and wide dribbling on command.
- Training peripheral vision.
- Dribbling the puck through a slalom.
- Dribbling the puck while doing tricks – kneeling, sitting, turning etc., both when skating forwards and backwards.
- Practicing other versions of puck handling – stroking, pushing, close and wide dribbling.
- Combining all versions of puck handling on a slalom course with tricks.
- Puck handling at close quarters and when being pressed (1:1).

The main mistakes in the technique

- Holding the stick with only one hand.
- The player doesn't handle the puck correctly, but knocks it forward too far and skates after it.
- The player only watches the puck.
- The player grasps the stick with the lower hand too far down or too high.
- The knob at the end of the stick is not held in the palm of the hand.
- The body is bent forward too far or it is held too upright.
- Same rhythm for dribbling as for skating.

The player breaking out with the puck using an evading maneuver

These individual game play actions are amongst the most important skills in ice hockey. Practicing them and perfecting them never ends. Getting round an opponent and outpacing him with a single individual game play action, together with the passing action form the main playing actions of the game and form at the same time the characteristics of team play.

Seen from the point of view of the methods in ice hockey, we speak of a player breaking out with the puck by using an evading action or sometimes by simply outpacing the opponent.

The most common versions of evading an opponent are:

GAME PLAY

- The evading maneuver.
- Forehand.
- Backhand.
- Evading maneuver to the side.
- Bringing the puck on.
- Tunneling.
- Dribbling round the opponent.

Evading maneuvers – forehand

This version is one of the most important individual skills for evading an opponent. It can be seen as an advantage for a player to be able to pass on immediately to a teammate or to carry out a goal shot (see Diagram 15).

The evading action starts with the player standing on both legs in front of an opponent, and with a slight movement of the puck to the backhand side, coupled with a faking movement of the shoulders and the head. As soon as the defending player reacts to these movements, the attacking player strokes the puck rapidly in front of the body on the forehand-side, and pushes off with his backhand-side leg. The player then sprints away followed by doing a cross-over. To protect the puck he uses his body and the inside of his leg. The stick is grasped in both hands and the blade is angled towards the puck. When going round the opponent, the puck is kept as far away from the body as possible. The head is held upright and the eyes are watching the opponent and his stick.

Diagram 15

Evading maneuvers – backhand

Practicing this version follows the same sequence as the previous evading maneuver. The technique is also very similar (see Diagram 16). The difference is that the first movement with the puck, done simultaneously with a faking movement of the shoulders and the head, is on the forehand side. The puck is pulled in front of the body on the backhand side (as far away from the body as possible). To protect the puck the player uses his body and inside leg again. First of all the stick is grasped in both hands. Later on, the lower hand leaves the stick and the player protects the puck with his stick. The edge of the blade of the stick must be firmly held flat on the ice and angled correctly towards the puck. Just as in the previous version and as important, the player sprints away (using the correct method of pushing off and accelerating) after getting round his opponent.

After learning both of the technical versions of the evading maneuver, the player must learn to gain an overview of the opponent's stick (right-handed or left-handed). From this you can then chose the best version to be used to get round an opponent. The faking movements and the sprint acceleration are emphasized in practice.

Diagram 16

GAME PLAY

Evading maneuvers – sideways

When it is better to evade the opponent down the side where he is holding his stick, then this version is used. The player alternates between a close dribbling movement to a wide version, and just in front of the defending player he pulls the puck rapidly to one side (with the forehand or the backhand) and attacks the opponent's stick with one of his legs. By virtue of his position he is covering the puck against being poked away from him and he goes off further round the opponent.

Evading maneuvers – pulling the puck back

This version is used against an opponent who is trying to play the puck with his stick. The attacking player pushes the puck as far as possible in front of the opponent (done best together with the faking maneuvers). When the opponent makes a move towards the puck, the player pulls the puck back as far as his skate. He then kicks the puck forwards onto the other side of the stick. It is important to accelerate immediately (breaking out from his opponent). This skill should be practiced, however, after the other previous versions have been learned.

Tunneling and playing round an opponent

Diagram 17

The attacking player can get round the opponent by **tunneling** the puck through between the leg nearest to the puck and his stick or between the legs. At the same time he skates round the opponent using faking movements.

One possible version of this is the so called **off-the-board** movement, done mainly by using the aid of the boards round the rink (see Diagram 17).

In order to make the tunneling or off-the-board effective, the attacking player must skate faster than the defender. Prior to either of these two versions, an evading faking movement (forehand or backhand) is often carried out.

FIRST STEPS FOR KIDS

Methodical tips

When training, the player learns not only the individual technical versions possible, but also when best to use them. Simultaneously, he learns to decide whether to take the puck on, shoot it or to pass it on to a teammate, who is in a better position.

- First of all, puck handling and breaking away with the puck is practiced.
- To start with, the players watch the puck; later they control it using peripheral vision and by gaining a feeling for the puck (for this several exercises can be used).
- For practicing puck handling, the exercise shown in Diagram 18 is very suitable. The player dribbles on the spot. Here, care is taken to ensure a correct hold on the stick. The shoulders are in front of the hips and the legs are bent at the knees. The stick is placed properly down on the ice and the head is held upright (the puck is controlled using peripheral vision).
- When dribbling, pushing or pulling the puck, skating skills must be coordinated with the handling of the puck.
- Simple exercises are chosen so that the techniques being carried out can be concentrated on. Only after the basic technique has been mastered, are more complex exercises (puck handling round obstacles, change of direction, skating backwards) put into practice.
- Breaking away round an opponent is done after various puck handling versions have been practiced.
- In training, standing objects and other immobile aids are used.
- The main prerequisite for a successful evading action is the faking movement done by the body and the stick.

Diagram 18

GAME PLAY

- When doing an evading maneuver, the player must increase his speed (generally and mainly by doing a cross-over).
- Standing objects can be used to practice tunneling and off-the-board maneuvers.
- First of all, you practice passively on the spot, then later with an active defending opponent (situation 1:1).
- The last step is control of the puck in close quarters and under threat.

Main technique faults

- Continually just watching the puck (the player only watches the puck and not the defending player).
- The evading maneuver is carried out too near or too far away from the defending player.
- Prior to carrying out an evading action the player doesn't carry out a faking movement.
- When doing an evading maneuver, the player doesn't accelerate and doesn't protect the puck sufficiently.

Passing and Receiving a Pass

The aim of passing is to move the puck in such a manner that the teammate can take the pass well. Passing calls for players, who are going to receive the pass, to be able to break out free. Mastering how to break out freely is one of the basic elements of learning an attacking combination and, generally, good game play.

The success of a pass is, of course, also dependent on the player, who is receiving the pass. He has to break away from the opponent and be able to control the puck safely. Good receipt of a pass makes for good puck control.

In passing techniques and receiving passes it depends on:

Passing technique
- Forehand – backhand.
- A pass flat over the ice – a pass, which comes over without touching the surface.

- A direct pass – a pass off-the-boards.
- Wrist flick pass (aka snap pass) – a hard pass (with power).

Receiving a pass
- Forehand.
- Backhand.
- Inaccurate pass.

For the group of six to eight year olds, the basic elementary skill is the flat forehand and backhand pass on the ice, as well as receiving a pass (forehand, backhand) in the frontal and the sideways position. The pass over the ice without touching it is practiced with only the best players.

The forehand snap pass

For this pass the player must adopt the correct basic position. The head is held upright and the eyes are following the stick of the player, who will receive the pass. The puck is behind the body, between the center of the blade and the beginning of the shaft. The stick is held in both hands and the player turns his shoulder in the direction of the pass. The blade of the stick is flat on the ice and angled towards the puck. The weight of the body is distributed equally over both legs, alternatively the weight can be centered over the leg, which is nearest to the puck (for a left-handed player – the left leg). At the time of the pass, the weight of the body is switched to the other leg (for a left-handed player – the right leg), and the puck is rotated off the blade leaving from the toe of the stick. The stick is followed through in the puck's direction (see Diagram 19).

Diagram 19

GAME PLAY

For a pass out of the standing position, the direction of the puck is towards the stick of the teammate. In the case that the pass is made on the move, the puck must be passed to allow for the speed of the teammate. The pass should be made using the snap pass (wrist shot) and not with a hard pass (power shot). The player looks at the aiming spot and not the puck. For young players, a common mistake is when the puck is played with the toe of the blade.

The backhand pass

The technique is similar to the forehand version. The difference lies, above all, in the basic position to be adopted and principally the requirement for accuracy when carrying it out.

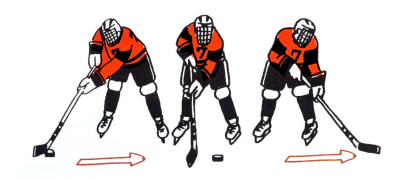

Diagram 20

The player stands sideways to his receiving teammate and the puck is in front of him in the center of the stick's blade. This is held on the ice and is angled towards the puck. The weight of the body is distributed equally over both legs, alternatively the weight can be centered over the rear leg (for a left-handed player – the right leg). At the time of the pass, the puck is pushed from the center of the stick in the direction of the teammate. The weight of the body is switched to the near leg. The arms are in front of the body, and, simultaneously the shoulders follow through, rotating in the puck's direction (see Diagram 20).

The flat pass

The flat pass is done with either a slow snap pass using the wrist (where the player has more time to prepare for the pass) or with a quick snap pass (where the pass is done without time for preparation when moving the puck forwards – particularly after an evading maneuver). The first version is smoother and is used for covering long distances. The second version is quicker. The puck is rotated minimally and can be passed to a teammate rapidly. It is also used when doing a so-called **spot pass**, that is to say where the pass is made into a pre-designated free area to be taken on by a teammate skating into the spot. The passer must judge the speed of the pass very accurately.

The flip pass

The flip pass is done in a situation where there is an obstacle (an opponent's stick etc.,) between the player with the puck and his teammate. Just as in the forehand or backhand pass it is carried out doing a short snap pass with the wrist. The blade of the stick is on the ice and is angled towards the puck. By using a short, smooth wrist movement, the puck rotates off the blade of the stick in a flat trajectory – this is important for the pass to be received. When the flip pass is done correctly it should land about 1 m away from the teammate's stick and its trajectory should be no more than 30 cm above the ice (see Diagram 21).

Diagram 21

GAME PLAY

Passing with the ice-skate

If the puck is close to the feet (ice-skates), it is not always possible to play it quickly with the stick. Sometimes, it is sufficient to change the direction of the puck by turning the ice-skate onto it (with the inside edge pointing in the direction of movement).

Receiving the puck on the forehand and the backhand

When receiving a pass on the forehand, the player stands at right angles to the puck. The head is held upright and the eyes are watching the puck. The blade of the stick is held on the surface of the ice. When taking the pass, relaxed movement of the wrist and the arms play an important role. At the moment when the pass comes, the stick is pushed partially forward (towards the puck) and the blade of the stick is held at right angles to the approaching puck. The weight of the body is distributed equally over both legs.

Just prior to the puck making contact with the blade, the player moves his stick backwards with the puck (however this movement is slower than the speed of the puck) thus braking it – cushioning it so to speak. The weight of the body transfers on to the leg nearest to the puck (for a left-handed player, the left leg). The aim is to keep the puck on the blade after receiving the pass in order to be able to carry out a pass straight away (see Diagram 22).

Diagram 22

The technique for receiving a pass on the forehand and the backhand is the same (see Diagram 23).

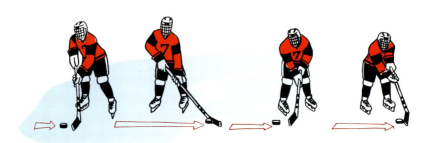

Diagram 23

After learning these basic techniques, you can go on to learn receiving a pass with the skate, out of the air, and by using the whole of the stick.

Receiving a pass using the skate

The player cushions (brakes) the puck either with the outside of the ice-skate (of the leg nearest the puck) or with the inside of the ice-skate. This version is used when the puck doesn't come in exactly or when it comes in from the rear (see Diagram 24).

Diagram 24

GAME PLAY

Receiving a pass out of the air

In the event that the puck flies low over the ice (at about knee-height), the player tries to knock it down vertically onto the ice with the blade of the stick.

When the puck comes in higher, it is knocked down with the open palm of the lower hand that normally holds the stick. When practicing, care should be taken to make sure that the hand doesn't close over the puck (known as cupping), but that it falls down vertically onto the blade of the stick (see Diagram 25).

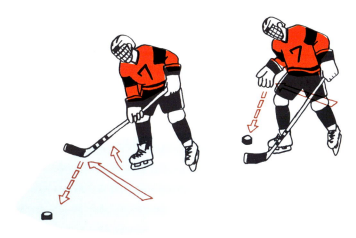

Diagram 25

Receiving a pass using the whole of the stick

If the puck is played too far in front of the player, the whole of the stick is used to receive the pass. The stick is held only in one hand and one knee is bent. It is important to have the whole of the stick with the blade on its side lying on the ice (see Diagram 26).

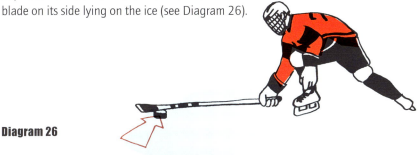

Diagram 26

Methodical tips

- Practice in the standing position with a forehand pass (of about 4-5 m).
- Later, the distance of the pass is increased and other pass receiving versions practiced (snap pass, hard pass, flat pass, flip pass, forehand, backhand).
- After learning how to give a pass and how to receive a pass standing still, these skills are now practiced with a partner on the move.
- Following on from this, practice on the move slowly (first of all on the forehand and then with the backhand).
- The next step in training is passing over a longer distance at a higher tempo. This is practiced in those playing areas where, in a game, such passing versions are possible (direct pass when going on the attack from the defense zone, drop passes with the puck at the end of an attack etc).
- The exercises include the body position both in the frontal as well as the sideways position.

Main technique faults

Passing
- The player doesn't aim at his teammate's blade of the stick (a blind pass).
- The player watches the puck and not the aim of the pass.
- The puck is struck too far towards the end of the blade of the stick.
- Wrong wrist movement.

Receiving a pass
- The stick isn't held down on the ice.
- The blade of the stick isn't held at right angles to the puck.
- The player holds the stick too tightly and firmly (the cushioning effect is lost in the wrists and the hands), and the puck bounces away off the blade.

GAME PLAY

Shooting Techniques

Shooting calls for a combination of many individual elements of movement carried out harmoniously, and therefore, in ice hockey it is a technically demanding action. A unison between ice skating, puck handling, shooting technique must be struck, at the same time being able to judge the game properly, being aware of what is happening, and inter alia, possessing the right amount of fitness. All the activities of the team, as well as each individual player, are focussed on gaining possession of the puck, controlling it and doing something worthwhile with it. This manifests itself in being able to score a goal.

The effectiveness of shooting at goal is influenced by a large number of parameters. The individual parameters should, however, not be considered in isolation. Of the more important of the parameters, the following are the ones, which lead considerably to influencing the chances of a goal:

a) **Technique** – a well learned perfect shooting technique not only represents a prerequisite for an optimum impulse in time, space and power, the accuracy of the shot also depends on it. The technique depends on the actual game situation. That is to say, particularly the relationship between the player and the puck, into which the goal and the goalie are brought. The ability to shoot well from a technical point of view allows the player to make a quick and precise shot at goal even in complicated situations (a shot on the turn, shooting under pressure and when skating very fast, shooting as you fall down, volley shots, shooting over a poor ice surface etc).

b) **Fitness** – besides technique, the effectiveness of a shot at goal is influenced by power in speed and strength. Also advantageous to this is body size (winning the one on one, larger radius of action possible, maintaining a good shooting position etc). Being fit also means, at the same time, that you don't get tired so quickly. Tiredness leads to negative results in the technical area, especially concerning speed and shooting accuracy. Negative results also appear in the tactical game play.

c) **Tactics** – the effectiveness of the shot at goal, of course, depends on the quick and correct appreciation of the game situation and how it is developed. This means choosing the right distance and moment to decide whether to shoot at goal or pass to a teammate, who is in a better position, as well as choosing the direction to shoot in. The most vulnerable goal areas are the upper and lower side corners of the goal i.e., those farthest away from the goalie. When close to the goal it is best to aim at the upper corners. From a medium or longer distance away, flat, hard shots are the most successful (including faking a shot in front of the goal mouth).

From a tactical point of view, shots at goal are usually most successful:
- After an evading maneuver (on the forehand or the backhand).
- When in close quarters.
- When in contact with the opponent.
- After making an evading movement in front of the goalie (as a flip shot or flat shot).
- By doing a faking movement or faking a shot.

d) **Mental** – a good mental aspect helps when shooting at goal, especially in challenging situations (e.g., taking a penalty).

The following aspects influence the effectiveness of shooting:
- Technique (being able to master the various different types of shots).
- Precision (only an aimed shot at an unmarked corner of the goal represents a danger).
- Speed of execution (shooting under pressure – both in space and time).
- Flexibility (mastering various different types of shots and choosing the most adequate of these for the job)

When shooting, the sequence is divided into four basic phases (see Diagram 27):
1) **Pulling the stick back** – controlling the movement of the stick correctly, which is along the line of where the puck will be shot.
2) **The swing** – this lasts until the blade of the stick comes into contact with the puck.
3) **Interaction** – the blade of the stick makes contact with the puck.
4) **Follow through** – this is the moment when the puck leaves the blade and the stick follows through in the direction of the shot.

GAME PLAY

Diagram 27

Concerning the speed of the puck, the most important phase is the interaction phase. This is when the blade of the stick accelerates the puck and the final speed of the puck depends on this acceleration.

The individual types of shot are divided into three groups according to their technical execution:

Forehand shots
- Wrist shot (quick, slow – pulling shot).
- Full shot.
- Flip shot.
- Slap shot.

Backhand shots
- Wrist shot.
- Full shot.

Other types of shot
- Intentional fake shot (tip-in).
- Rebound shot.
- Volley shot, on the turn, when falling etc.

FIRST STEPS FOR KIDS

Forehand – quick wrist shot

This version of the shot is one of the basic skills for players of all age groups and therefore has priority in training. Using the quick wrist shot the player can take a well-aimed shot at goal even under pressure. The technique is similar to the passing technique using the wrist. The hands grip the stick (shoulder width apart) and the puck handling are both approximately the same. When the situation allows, the lower hand can be pushed further down, giving more power. The speed of the shot depends on good coordination between the arms and the wrists.

The blade of the stick angled against it moves the puck and this takes place to the side of the body on a level with the rear leg (for a left-handed player, the left leg). With the stick pushing hard on the puck and by using the arms, the player (for example with a left-handed player) puts his weight at the same time on the other leg, i.e., the right leg. The left leg balances the movements of the arms and the stick, so that the latter is held diagonally to the rear and sideways. The player grasps the stick by the left hand firmly in the middle of the shaft and, by using a quick wrist movement, the blade is angled away from the puck. At the same time, this hand determines the direction (and accuracy) of the shot. For the whole of the movement, the following sequence is important: upper body – arms – wrist – stick – blade. The puck leaves the blade from the middle via the toe. In this version, importantly, the correct impulse of force follows from the upper body, arms and hands on to the stick (see Diagram 28).

It is a mistake to make an incorrect and too weak a wrist movement, which is caused by not holding the stick with the lower hand firmly enough.

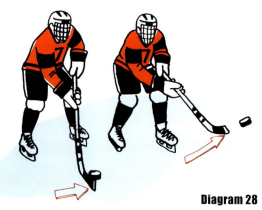

Diagram 28

GAME PLAY

Forehand shot – slow wrist shot (pulling shot)

This version demands more power and, therefore, is not taught to the very young players. In comparison to the quick wrist shot, the puck is more behind the body (behind the rear leg). You can hold the stick wider than shoulder width. The blade of the stick is angled towards the puck and during the interaction phase the puck is held longer on the blade than in the previous shooting method. The puck leaves the rear part of the blade out over the toe. In practice, it is also important that the blade of the stick follows through in the intended direction after the shot has been made. The basics for correct technical execution are taking a firm grasp of the stick with the lower hand and that the force comes from the upper body via the arms and the wrist on to the stick (see Diagram 29).

Here, also the sequence of the individual movements is important: upper body – arms – wrist – stick – blade.

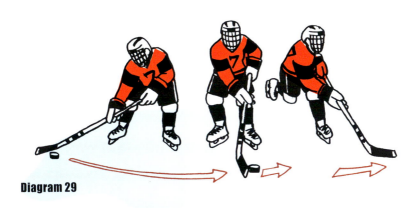

Diagram 29

Forehand shot – full shot

The puck is moved along using the rear part (heel) of the blade. Prior to actually making the shot the stick momentarily leaves the puck. The blade is twisted flat and the bottom edge is raised up a little from the ice. The swinging movement that follows hits the puck by using the middle of the blade, and the rotation of the stick ends at that moment. At the moment when the blade strikes the puck it is important to have a firm grip with the lower hand. For a left-handed player, for example, the weight of the body is over the left leg. The other leg (the right one) carries out a balancing movement rearwards and sideways (see Diagram 30).

Diagram 30

The trajectory of the puck depends on the angle of the blade as it is hit. A higher angle gives a high trajectory over the ice (see Diagram 31).

Diagram 31

Flip shot

This version requires no preparation and therefore it can be done quickly and flexibly. The puck is usually struck by the middle and the toe of the blade. As before, the height of the puck's trajectory is determined by the angle of the blade to it.

GAME PLAY

Slap shot

This version – the slap shot – is the one that gives the puck its highest speed amongst all the other versions. As a disadvantage is the fact that it is not so accurate and it requires considerable preparatory time (for the pull-back of the stick). This gives the defender and the goalie a certain amount of advantage. No way should this version of the shot be taught to children in the youngest age group.

The stick is held with the shoulders wider apart (the lower hand is further down) than in the wrist shot. Holding the stick firmly with the lower hand plays an important role. At the moment when the stick strikes the puck, it is level with the center of the axis of the body (frontal or sideways). When pulling the stick back it is brought to the rear and upwards (to just above shoulder height). After the swing back down of the stick, the puck is struck by the middle to the heel of the blade. The full follow through of the stick in the direction of the shot is also important. In order to balance the body and the arm movements at the moment of the puck being struck, the left leg (for a left-handed player) is thrust hard to the rear.

The trajectory of the puck, again, is dependent on the angle of the blade against the puck (at the time that it leaves the blade)(see Diagram 32). In order to execute a flat shot, the angle should be as large as possible.

A common mistake with beginners is where they strike the ice with the blade or the trajectory is too high, because they have struck it with only the toe of the blade.

Diagram 32

Backhand wrist shot

This version is one of the most demanding shooting techniques. Practicing this must start right from the youngest age groups. Practicing this basic shot is done, first of all, in a sideways position. Besides this it is best to do it when moving slowly – preferably when doing a curve. The puck is moved along by the side of the body (behind the rear leg) using the heel and the center of the blade of the stick, which is angled towards the puck. The role of the movement of the lower hand is important here. It pulls the blade with the puck forwards rapidly. The arm is stretched out and is not bent. The upper arm, however, is bent and moves across the body to the front. Rotating the shoulders and the body accelerates the movement of the stick, while the weight is transferred across. The movement of the legs also plays an important role (see Diagram 33).

Diagram 33

Basic rules of correct shooting techniques:
- Peripheral control of the puck and the target.
- Firm grasp of the stick (mainly with the lower hand on the middle of the shaft).
- The hand grasping the stick determines the direction of the shot (accuracy).
- The hand holding the end of the stick executes an assisting movement.
- Correct sequence of the movements: upper body – arms – wrist – stick – blade.
- The puck should rotate (roll) off along the blade and have a flat trajectory.

GAME PLAY

Methodical tips/Training emphasis

Practicing how to shoot begins after the introduction to the technique of passing. Training concentrates, to start with, on the quick wrist shot. The training method is just the same as used in learning the wrist pass in principle. Training is divided up as follows:

- Demonstration, explanation and description of the shooting technique being taught.
- Practicing while standing still (later at targets) – (see Diagram 34).

Diagram 34

- Practice standing still in front of the goal.
- Shooting while on the move.
- Skate towards the goal – finish off with a shot at goal.
- Receive a pass – dribble – take a shot.
- Receive a pass – do a straight direct shot at goal.
- Shooting off the rebound.
- Repeated shots.
- Taking a shot while under pressure.

Advice on shooting training

Shooting training should be carried out at targets, i.e., from the beginning accuracy should be emphasized. One possible target is a mark made on the board around the rink – the outline of the goal. Players should aim at the free corners of the goal. Young players should practice shooting using a direct shot as often as

HOCKEY
FIRST STEPS FOR KIDS

possible. This system allows for a number of goals to be used. At the same time, flat as well as high shots should be practiced. After a short phase in training from on the spot, the exercises should be carried out on the move. Besides the accuracy of the shot, the power behind the shot (dependent on how far away the goal is) is also to be taken care of. In the first phases of training the technique is learned, then later the accuracy, followed up finally by the power behind the shot.

As soon as the players have developed the necessary power in their wrists and can master the basic technicalities, they can practice the wrist shot successfully – **doing quick wrist shots**. This version should be the main emphasis of the training. Nevertheless, practicing the full shot and the backhand shots is also important.

After learning the basics of the technique, the exercises should be carried out to include a factor of pressure. There are several types of pressure – space, timing, threat from the opponent, mental pressure, tiredness etc.

Besides accuracy and power, the player needs the skill to be able to control the puck on the rebound, in order to shoot again, to fake out with the flying puck or to be able to react correctly in a one-on-one situation in front of the opponent's goal mouth. Nevertheless, the most important skill to have is to be able to exploit the opportunity gained to have a shot at goal.

Shooting practice is the most important of all the training exercises. It is an endless process, as much from the standpoint of age (from the youngest players up to grown-ups) as well as from the standpoint of performance (from beginner to national team player). In practice, it is advantageous to carry the exercises out with the maximum amount of variety (different degrees of difficulty, large selection).

GAME PLAY

Marking

This term means a defense activity, done with the aim of bringing the puck under control or to slow down an opponent's attack. Attacking an opponent in possession of the puck is the basis of defensive play. The quality of the attack plays a decisive role for the whole game. A prerequisite for mastering all the defense skills is to be able to skate well.

Defense can be carried out using the stick, the body or both. For the group of six to eight year olds it is recommended to teach them the basic technique of using the stick to tackle the puck away from the opponent. Straight away, this plays an important role because of the fact that following on from winning the puck, a push-off start and a pass have to be made.

The basic types of tackling the puck away with the stick are:
- Hooking out the puck.
- Sweep check.
- Hitting the puck away.
- Lifting the stick.
- Pushing the stick away.
- Striking the bottom half of the opponent's stick (against the puck).

All the defensive actions with the stick occur when the defending player is not in close contact with the opponent in possession of the puck. It is important that the player moves correctly and, in relation to the opponent, takes up a suitable position. Said in other words, if the defense using the stick fails, the defending player must be in a position so that he can still defend.

Practicing the individual skills is done according to the position of the defending player. He is standing either frontally or sideways to the opponent.

If he is standing in a frontal position, he skates backwards and is in a position between the opponent and his own goal.

Defending player is in a sideways position:
- When the opponent attacks, he skates towards him in a curve and makes him move from a middle course on to the side by the boards (see Diagram 35).

Diagram 35

- Regaining possession of the puck from the opposition (back-checking), when the player is skating towards his own goal and comes level with the opponent to take the puck off him (see Diagram 36).

Diagram 36

GAME PLAY

Hooking out the puck

This version of taking possession of the puck is used when the defenseman is skating backwards. He holds the stick only in one hand (the upper) and watches the puck peripherally. It is important that as he does this he has the correct position – arms shoulder width and legs bent to allow a quick push-off and a change in direction in case his attempt is unsuccessful.

The stick is held, with arm bent, in front of the body. At an opportune moment, when the attacking player is near enough, the defenseman hooks the stick quickly in the direction of the puck and against the opponent's stick so that he hits the puck with his blade. This movement has to be done merely by stretching out the bent arm (see Diagram 37).

Diagram 37

When doing this it is important to maintain a position, from which the player can continue playing on without a problem.

Sweep check

This version is used in the event that the defending player comes up behind the player with the puck. The stick is held in the upper hand so that the shaft lies as far as possible down along the ice. The blade of the stick is also flat on its side on the ice with the toe pointing towards the puck. At an opportune moment, the defender kneels down on one leg, and at the same time he pushes his stick forward so that he can hook out the puck with the area of the stick between the shaft and the blade (see Diagram 38).

HOCKEY
FIRST STEPS FOR KIDS

Diagram 38

It is important that you don't kneel down too early and that the blade of the stick is flat down on the ice.

However, this version should only be used when there is a good chance of success. Otherwise the player will find himself in a very poor position to execute further defense maneuvers.

Hitting the puck away

This skill is similar to the previous one. It is generally used when the defending player is on the move and is skating frontally towards the opponent with the puck or is in front of him.

The player holds the stick, as before, in one (the upper) hand and he attempts, by skating in a fast curve, to strike the puck. Similarly, the stick should be lying as flat as possible on the surface of the ice. The puck should be struck at a point on the stick between the shaft and the blade. Once again the player kneels down on one knee while his other leg is either also bent or stretched out backwards or sideways (see Diagram 39).

GAME PLAY

Diagram 39

The defenseman should not try to do the movement too quickly, as by doing this he must avoid loosing his balance and losing contact with the opponent. Young players must be taught that if the move is unsuccessful, they must continue trying to defend.

Lifting the stick

The use of the stick here is suitable for situations when the defending player comes up behind the player with the puck (see Diagram 40 or 41). A prerequisite is, however, that he is skating faster than the opponent.

As soon as he comes up behind (or in front of) the opponent, he lifts the opponent's stick (at the lower extremity) and then quickly puts his own stick down back onto the ice in order to take on the puck. To protect the puck he uses the leg that is nearest and a little forward of the opponent. On gaining the puck, the player should set off to make a breakaway from the opponent.

Diagram 40

HOCKEY
FIRST STEPS FOR KIDS

Diagram 41

Pushing the stick away

This version is used in a one-on-one situation to prevent the puck being received. The defending player places his own stick over the opponent's stick (done best by using the lower part of the shaft of the stick – not the blade). Using a sharp pressure, the player tries to prevent the opponent moving his stick. It is important when doing this (above all, when done by young players) that not only the arms but also the upper body are used with some force (see Diagram 42).

Diagram 42

GAME PLAY

Striking the bottom half of the opponent's stick (against the puck)

This version is for use when the player is skating parallel to the opponent dribbling the puck.

When the opponent has the puck (but on the other side to the defending player), the defenseman makes a short strike on the attacker's stick. In order to make this attack efficiently, the opponent's stick must be struck in the immediate vicinity of the blade of the stick (see Diagram 43).

Diagram 43

Methodical tips/Training emphasis

- The players practice the defensive movements with the stick on the spot – proper execution is to be emphasized.
- In pairs (moving slowly) – the attacking player dribbles the puck without trying to outpace the defending player, who carries out various versions of gaining puck possession: either frontally to the opponent or when skating parallel with the opponent.

HOCKEY
FIRST STEPS FOR KIDS

- In pairs (moving slowly) – the attacking forward tries to get round the defender, either by controlled dribbling or an evading movement. The defender tries to get the puck off him by using different means.
- The attacking forward tries to get round the defender from a close quarter position.
- Gaining puck possession using exercises and games.
- The defender skates along with the player in puck possession and tries to continually attack him with his stick. He must carry on even after an unsuccessful attempt.
- Exercises and games, following on from which, after the puck has been gained, push-offs and the beginning of attacks are practiced.

Main technique faults

- When in contact with the opponent, movement is not coordinated sufficiently – indecisiveness.
- Wrong choice of version to gain possession of the puck.
- Infringements of the rules.
- Gaining possession of the puck doesn't represent a signal for the immediate start of an attack.
- After a failed attempt, further defense is not possible.

MINI HOCKEY

As mentioned already, playing at close quarters in a small area is a firm feature of every training period. In the first few years of training, various little games are combined with mini hockey. As the children get older, and as their skills improve, later on mini hockey should predominate in the session. For eight year olds it takes on an important role. Therefore, here, we lay out some basic rules for tournaments for the 7-8 year olds. However, rules vary from country to country, so you should check with your local federations for the official rules.

Pitch
- Matches are played in individual zones, which are separated from each other by removable boards or a normal hose.
- Standard sized goal mouths are used (as for ice hockey rules) and are placed on the face-off circles (as near as possible to the sideboards, but allowing room to be able to play behind the goal).
- The players, who are not taking part in the game at any moment, sit out on the player's benches.

Equipment
- All players wear the full equipment.
- The puck used is one third lighter.

Teams
- For each match the maximum number of players is 13 (one goalie and 12 players).
- Play is carried out in the zones 4:4 (for a practice match 5:5, 3:3 and 2:2 is recommended).

Timing and Player changeovers (substitutions)
- Each match lasts 3 x 15 minutes 'pure' playing time.
- Player changeover occurs periodically after 60 seconds (90 seconds can also be used).

HOCKEY
FIRST STEPS FOR KIDS

MINI HOCKEY

Referee
- A referee controls the game.
- The game is always started from the center of the playing area.

Rule infringements
- Body checking or hip checking is not allowed.
- Player changeovers while play is in progress (flying changes) are not allowed.
- Other infringements are punished as in ice hockey.

Punishments
- Three infringements against the rules are followed by a penalty shot.
- After each infringement, the referee stops the game and the punishment reported to the official recorder.
- The game continues with a face-off in the middle of the playing area – the player is not sent to the penalty box.

Penalty shot
- Players chosen by the trainer carry these out.
- The player skates from his own goal up to the middle of the playing area to take it.
- The other players are behind the goal line while the shot is being taken.

Offside and icing the puck or the 2 line rule
- These rules do not exist in mini hockey.

Face-off
- The face-off is done in the center of the playing area (each time after a goal shot or in the event that the puck is hit off the playing area).
- The players adopt the same positions as in the full game.

Timekeeper
- He keeps the play timing and indicates the right time for the periods and when to put in substitutes by giving an acoustic signal.

TRAINING EXAMPLES FOR A SIX YEAR OLD

Number: 14
Date: October
Total time: 60 minutes
Location: Ice hockey Stadium
Age Group: Six year olds
Number of players: 30
Number of trainers: 4
Training aim: Games, Skating

Content of Training Unit

Beginning:
- Moving around freely, greeting the children, achievement of a positive atmosphere.

Warm-up and Main part:
- Catching the rope: The trainer pulls a rope behind him. When all the players are holding on to the rope, the 'train leaves the station'. The trainer is the locomotive, which pulls the trucks. On the command "Bridge!" the players do a knees bend; when the command is "Tunnel!" they stay in that position. The trainer skates through different curves to give training for balance.
- "Pumping" – bend the knees – stand up – bend the knees.
- "Stork" – standing on one leg, bending the upper body over to the side and changing the weight of the body on to that side; holding the leg out to one side.
- "Frog" – hopping from a knees bend position into another knees bend position.
- Skating training – skate forwards round the rink.
- Time out and breathing exercises.
- The trainers swing the rope (about 5m long) – the players skate underneath or jump over it.
- Doing the "stork" while skating forwards.

TRAINING EXAMPLES

- "Bear" – skating forwards, swinging the body from one side to the other (changing the center of balance of the body).
- Doing the "frog" while skating forwards.
- Skating training – skating forwards.
- Time out and breathing exercises.
- Jumping over the "live rope".
- Competition – form two teams; on a signal they all let go of the rope, skate around their own goal and come back.
- Doing the "stork", "bear", "frog" – skating forwards with hands clasped behind the back.
- Time out and breathing exercises.
- Skating training – with hands still.
- "Lasso" – the trainer twirls the rope round and tries to wrap it round the players.

Conclusion:
- Form "statues" – skate around freely and on a command all stand still and are not allowed to move.
- Time out and breathing exercises.
- Altogether for a farewell – assessment (positive) – motivation for the next period.

Notes:
- The whole team is divided up into three groups and all do the same exercises. The full time for the individual exercises cannot be pre-determined. One has to remain flexible and react to the actual situation and the children's concentration. During the training session, time must be allowed to take a drink and to retie the laces on the skates (this is also the case in other training units).

HOCKEY
FIRST STEPS FOR KIDS

Number: 22	**Age Group:** Six year olds
Date: November	**Number of players:** 60
Total time: 60 minutes	**Number of trainers:** 5
Location: Ice hockey Stadium	**Training aim:** Skating games

Content of Training Unit

Warm-up:
- Greeting, motivation pep talk for the training, stretching exercises.
- Skating freely as laid down by the trainer.

Main part:
- Training at stations (five stands); change round after 10 minutes.
- A trainer (assistant) is at each stand.

Stations/Stands:
1) Mini hockey.
2) Games – catching games, races.
3) Partner catching games.
4) The "reds" and the "whites" from different starting positions (catching game).
5) Relay team races – skating forwards, slalom backwards.

Conclusion:
- Skating freely around with the trainer.
- Breathing exercises and relaxing the muscles.
- Feedback, evaluating the training session.

Notes:
- The lads have passed a basic course in ice skating.
- The training session takes place using station/stands, so that the children can be grouped in categories according to their differing skills.

TRAINING EXAMPLES

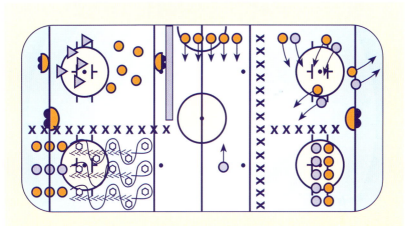

Diagram 44

105

HOCKEY
FIRST STEPS FOR KIDS

Number: 27	**Age Group:** Six year olds
Date: November	**Number of players:** 30
Total time: 60 minutes	**Number of trainers:** 3
Location: Ice hockey Stadium	**Training aim:** Skating

Content of Training Unit

Beginning:
- Greeting, motivation pep talk, stretching exercises.

Warm-up and Main part:
- "Snowball fight" – without sticks. The children throw balls of paper or light balls at each other, which may only be picked up by going into a knees bend posture. On a command – who can pick up the most balls?
- Skating on the spot – doing squats, jumping sideways from one leg on to the other, hopping on one leg – mimicking a bird "sparrow" on the spot and when skating.
- Ice skating training – with the stick.
- Time out and breathing exercises.
- "Throwing the ball to the opposition" – the red line forms a barrier between two teams, and this cannot be stepped over. The aim is to throw as many balls as possible into the opponent's half. The team with the least balls in their half are the winners.
- "Jet fighter" – skating without the stick, with the body leaning forward and the arms stretched out to the sides.
- Ice-skating training forwards – with the stick.
- Time out and breathing exercises.
- Skating through a "danger zone" – the children skate between the blue lines in a neutral zone, and try to miss being hit by balls being thrown at them. Change of exercise: The "jet fighters" skate in curves with their bodies bending over sideways. The trainer looks for the fastest "jet fighter" and for those who skate a curve the best.
- Ice skating training – higher speed, with the stick.

TRAINING EXAMPLES

- Time out and breathing exercises.
- The game with the ring – the children skate with a ring on the end of the stick, which is held the wrong way round. Those without a ring try to get one. Everyone plays against everyone else on the whole rink. There are about 4 rings too few amongst the players.

Conclusion:
- Time out and breathing exercises.
- Meeting – assessment, calming down session, motivation.

HOCKEY
FIRST STEPS FOR KIDS

Number: 40	**Age Group:** Six year olds
Date: December	**Number of players:** 30
Total time: 60 minutes	**Number of trainers:** 3
Location: Ice hockey Stadium	**Training aim:** Skating forwards, doing curves

Content of Training Unit

Beginning:
- Greeting the children, motivation.

Warm-up and Main part:
- "Bringing the others off balance" – the trainer (or the players) without sticks try to topple over and unbalance the other players, who have got sticks. Any player who is toppled over, lays his stick down and joins in. The winner is the last player holding a stick.
- Competition: Who can jump over the most sticks laid on the ice in various positions?
- Competition: Who can skate fastest to the trainer? Improvement of the forwards skating technique.
- Time out and breathing exercises.
- Skating in a curve – without a stick (see Diagram 45).
- Skating through a "danger zone" – the children skate between the blue lines, while others try to hit them with sticks and tennis balls.
- Skating forwards – skating with the knee bent and coming up into an upright stance and changing sides.
- Time out and breathing exercises.
- Skating curves – without sticks.
- Competition: Who can collect up the most tennis balls from the ice? The balls can only be picked up one at a time and put in a bucket. The trainer throws them all back on the ice.
- "Motor bike competition" – the stick is held as a handlebar. After one circuit to the left do breathing exercises and then a circuit to the right.
- Time out and breathing exercises.

TRAINING EXAMPLES

- Skating curves with the stick; the stick serves as a 'rudder'.
- Game: Each against the other with a tennis ball.

Conclusion:
- "Figure skating" – dancing on the ice.

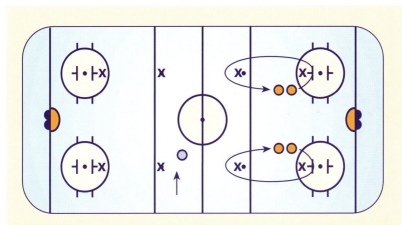

Diagram 45

HOCKEY
FIRST STEPS FOR KIDS

Number: 53	**Age Group:** Six year olds
Date: January	**Number of players:** 30
Total time: 60 minutes	**Number of trainers:** 4
Location: Ice hockey Stadium	**Training aim:** Skating cross-over forwards

Content of Training Unit

Beginning:
- Greeting, motivation.

Warm-up and Main part:
- "The devil": Some children have a skipping rope fastened to the rear of their bodies (as a 'tail'). The other children try to take the skipping rope away. Whoever manages this is the new 'devil'.
- The "leg trip": The trainer or a player with a stick trips other players up. The fallen player takes the stick and helps with tripping further.
- Skating forwards – round the rink. On a signal they skate in a curve to the boards in the other direction; this is repeated.
- Time out and breathing exercises.
- Doing the forwards cross-over – round the face-off circle, without a stick – preparatory exercises for the cross-over.
- "Deep frozen": A group of players (without sticks and grouped by tricot color or helmets) has to catch the others. Those being caught have got their sticks. Any player caught has to stand still – 'deep frozen' and he forms a 'bridge' (see Diagram 46). The others can save themselves by skating underneath the bridge.
- Time out and breathing exercises.
- Skating with a forwards cross-over – round the face-off circle, with a stick.
- "The sheep and the wolf": The sheep have to skate a circuit to get to their pen. One player, as the wolf, skates off afterwards and tries to overtake as many players as possible ('gobbling up the sheep').
- Doing the forwards cross-over – round the face-off circle, with a stick.

TRAINING EXAMPLES

- Competition: The "tow truck". One player tows another, who is holding onto two sticks. The competition takes place between the goal line and the red line. The players run back on their own.
- Game with rings – on the whole rink, 15: 15 (players) with five rings.
- Time out and breathing exercises.
- Game with tennis balls – done in the same way as the game with the rings.

Conclusion:
- A game of catch.
- Time out and breathing exercises.
- Meeting, assessment, motivation.

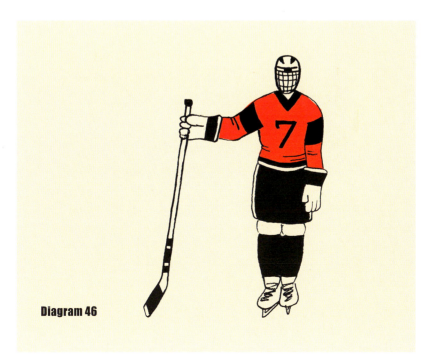

Diagram 46

HOCKEY
FIRST STEPS FOR KIDS

Number: 56	**Age Group:** Six year olds
Date: January	**Number of players:** 60
Total time: 75 minutes	**Number of trainers** 6
Location: Ice hockey Stadium	**Training aim:** Skating, individual games

Content of Training Unit

Beginning:
- Greeting, skating – chasing games.

Main part:
- Exercises at six stations/stands with a changeover every 10 minutes.
- On each stand there is a trainer (assistant).

Stations/Stands
1) Backwards cross-over.
2) Skating forwards without the puck – brake, turn, kneel down, jump up, go into a knee bend etc.
3) Skating backwards – brake, kneel down, turn.
4) Puck handling, shooting and skating on.
5) Puck handling.
6) Forwards cross-over.

Conclusion:
- Skating freely around with the trainer.
- Breathing exercises and loosening the muscles.
- Meeting, assessment of the training.

Notes:
- The players have already done a basic course in ice-skating.
- The training unit is done in stations/stands, so that it is possible to divide the children according to their differing skills.
- When changing round stations, a time out should be made to have a drink and check the equipment.

112

TRAINING EXAMPLES

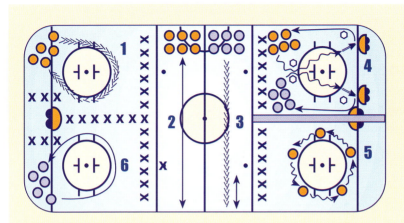

Diagram 47

HOCKEY
FIRST STEPS FOR KIDS

Number: 66	**Age Group:** Six year olds
Date: February	**Number of players:** 30
Total time: 60 minutes	**Number of trainers:** 4
Location: Ice hockey Stadium	**Training aim:** Curves, Cross-overs

Content of Training Unit

Beginning:
- Greeting, motivation, skating around freely.

Warm-up and Main part:
- "Bringing the others off balance" – see Training Unit No 40.
- The "leg trip" – see Training Unit No 53.
- Time out and breathing exercises.
- Doing the cross-over round the face-off circle – the circle becomes tighter and tighter (see Diagram 48a). As the circle gets tighter the legs have to do more cross-overs. With enlargement of the circle the speed is higher.
- Skating a curve – carry on with the cross-over, without a stick.
- Catching game: one-on one without a stick – you catch by touching with the hand; skate as many curves as possible, practicing the cross-over.
- Doing the cross-over in a spiral (see Diagram 48b) skating forwards, do the cross-over forwards, skating on and vice versa.
- Time out and breathing exercises.
- Skating a curve – with a cross-over; this is done with the stick.
- "Copy cat": the first player skates as he likes forwards (in curves and using the cross-over). The second player follows him and copies his movements.
- Time out and breathing exercises.
- Skating round the rink – on a signal do a curve towards the boards with a cross-over at the end.
- "Bringing the other player off balance" – 1:1 in a game zone so that you have to do the cross-over a lot.
- The "leg trip" – 1:1 in a game zone so that you have to do the cross-over a lot.

TRAINING EXAMPLES

- Time out and breathing exercises.
- Game with the rings – in single game zones.
- Game with the tennis balls – in single game zones.

Conclusion:
- Catching game – all the players catch the trainer.
- Time out and breathing exercises.
- Closing meeting, calming down, assessment, motivation for the next session.

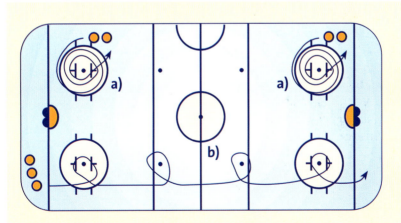

Diagram 48

HOCKEY
FIRST STEPS FOR KIDS

Number: 72	**Age Group:** Six year olds
Date: March	**Number of players:** 60
Total time: 60 minutes	**Number of trainers:** 5
Location: Ice hockey Stadium	**Training aim:** Skating, mini hockey

Content of Training Unit

Warm-up:
- Greeting, motivation.
- Catching game.

Main part:
- Exercises at five stations/stands, change round after 10 minutes. A trainer or an assistant is at each of the stations/stands.

Stations/Stands:
1) Mini hockey.
2) Ice-skating with a partner – pushing, pulling each other etc.
3) Doing the cross-over forwards, backwards.
4) Puck handling – in a slalom course with obstacles.
5) Ice-skating without the puck – braking, turning, kneeling.

Conclusion:
- Play the game "statues"; skate round freely and on a signal all stand still without moving.
- Breathing exercise, loosen the muscles.
- Meeting, training assessment.

Notes:
- The players have already carried out a basic course in ice-skating.
- The training unit is done in stations/stands, so that it is possible to divide the children according to their differing skills.
- When changing round stations, a time out should be made to have a drink and check the equipment.

116

TRAINING EXAMPLES

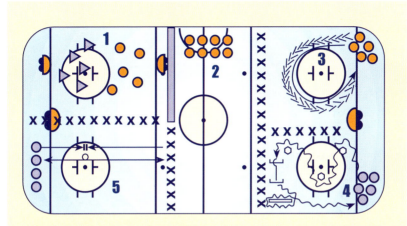

Diagram 49

TRAINING EXAMPLES FOR A SEVEN YEAR OLD

Number: 8	**Age Group:** Seven year olds
Date: August	**Number of players:** 30
Total time: 60 minutes	**Number of trainers:** 3
Location: Ice hockey Stadium	**Training aim:** Puck handling

Content of Training Unit

Beginning:
- Greeting, motivation.
- Catching game.

Warm-up and Main part:
- Catching game 1:1.
- Puck handling:
a) On the spot.
b) On the spot with stamping of the feet ("the hedgehog").
c) Doing the "stork" on the spot.
d) Turning round on the spot.

- Skating forwards – twisting the stick round the body, pushing it through the legs forwards.
- Puck handling when skating – pushing the puck on, dribbling close. Competition: Who doesn't drop the puck?
- "Stealing" the puck: All the players do puck handling. One player, without a stick, tries to take the puck away from them. The player, whose puck has been stolen, puts his stick down and goes off to steal pucks also.
- Forwards cross-over – in a spiral to the left then to the right (see Diagram 50a).
- Forwards cross-over – doing a snake (see Diagram 50b).

TRAINING EXAMPLES

- "Deep frozen": The player, who has been caught, kneels down. He can be freed by doing a circuit of cross-overs around him.
- Game with the rings – in single game zones.
- Play a game with the puck 2:2.
- Play a game in a game zone e.g., 2 x 2:2 or 3 x 2:2.

Conclusion:
- Skating freely with the trainer.
- Stretching and breathing exercises.
- Meeting, training assessment.

Notes:
- During the training unit, fit in stretching and breathing exercises.
- As required take time out between the individual exercises for a drink and a check of the equipment.

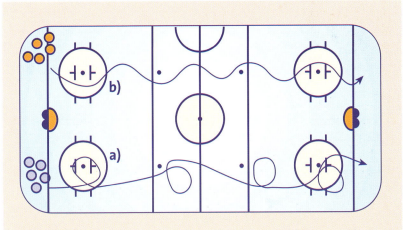

Diagram 50

HOCKEY
FIRST STEPS FOR KIDS

Number: 12	**Age Group:** Seven year olds
Date: September	**Number of players:** 60
Total time: 60 minutes	**Number of trainers:** 6
Location: Ice hockey Stadium	**Training aim:** Skating, individual game skills

Content of Training Unit

Warm-up:
- Greeting, motivation.
- Skating around freely with the trainer, stretching exercises.

Main part:
- Exercises at five stations, changeover after 10 minutes. On each stand there is a trainer or an assistant.

Stations/Stands:
1) Mini hockey.
2) Puck handling.
3) Passing on the move.
4) Puck handling on the forwards cross-over.
5) Puck handling using the wrist shot.

Conclusion:
- Game – "statues": Skating around freely and on a signal everyone stands still without moving.
- Breathing out, loosening the muscles, stretching exercises.
- Meeting, training assessment.

Notes:
- The players have already done a basic course in ice-skating.
- The training unit is conducted in stations, so that the children can be divided up into groups according to their individual skills.
- When changing stations, a time out should be allowed for to take a drink and check the equipment.

TRAINING EXAMPLES

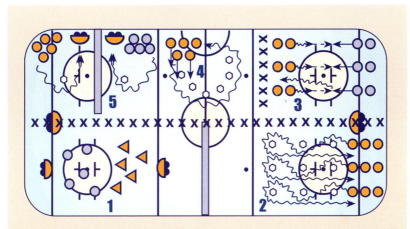

Diagram 51

HOCKEY
FIRST STEPS FOR KIDS

Number: 18	**Age Group:** Seven year olds
Date: September	**Number of players:** 30
Total time: 70 minutes	**Number of trainers:** 3
Location: Ice hockey Stadium	**Training aim:** Puck handling

Content of Training Unit

Beginning:
- Greeting, motivation.
- Game – " The sheep and the wolf".

Warm-up and Main part:
- "Deep frozen": The player, who has been caught lies on the ice. He can be freed by being jumped over.
- Puck handling training:
  - On the spot – close dribbling.
  - Wide dribbling.
  - Close – wide dribbling.
  - Round the gloves.
  - While stamping the feet – "the hedgehog","stork". Doing turns on the spot.
- Puck handling on the move.
  - Round the rink.
  - Step by step try out all the versions.
- "Playing for the pucks": Half of the players are doing puck handling. The others want to get them off them. The game takes place on the whole of the rink.
- Ice-skating backwards. When learning this, the methodical sequence with preparatory exercises should be used.
- Ice-skating forwards in curves following on with cross-overs (skate a figure of eight).
- "Deep frozen": The player, who has been caught makes a "bridge" with his stick (see Diagram 46 in Training Unit No. 53 – Six year olds).

122

TRAINING EXAMPLES

- Game with the pucks: In a single playing zone, play 1:1 with a puck (i.e., in the playing zone they play e.g., 4 x 1:1, 3 x 1:1 etc).

Conclusion:
- Skating freely with the trainer.
- Stretching and breathing exercises.
- Meeting, training assessment.

Notes:
- As required take time out between the individual exercises for a drink and a check of the equipment.

HOCKEY
FIRST STEPS FOR KIDS

Number: 28	**Age Group:** Seven year olds
Date: October	**Number of players:** 30
Total time: 60 minutes	**Number of trainers:** 3
Location: Ice hockey Stadium	**Training aim:** Individual game skills, backwards cross-over

Content of Training Unit

Beginning:
- Greeting, motivation.
- Copy cat skating with the trainer, stretching and breathing exercises.

Warm-up and Main part:
- "Bringing the others off balance": All the players without sticks. A nominated player tries to push the others off balance. The ones that topple over join in.

  Puck handling
  - On the move, "stork".
  - Short and long dribbling.
  - Close and wide dribbling.

- Game – "Playing for the pucks": Half of the players have pucks. The others want to get them off them. The game takes place in one of the playing zones.
- Backwards cross-over – around the face-off circle.
- Forwards cross-over – left round the face-off circle. On a command do a turn round to the right with right footed cross-overs etc.
- "Bringing the others off balance": 1:1, on a signal they all do a cross-over circuit to the side and then the game carries on.

  Game with the pucks:
  - In single playing zones.
  - 2:2 with a puck (i.e., 3 x 3:2, 2 x 2:2 etc).

TRAINING EXAMPLES

Conclusion:
- Catching game : Whoever is caught, kneels down.
- Stretching and breathing exercises.
- Meeting, training assessment.

Notes:
- During the training unit, fit in stretching and breathing exercises.
- As required take time out between the individual exercises for a drink and a check of the equipment.

HOCKEY
FIRST STEPS FOR KIDS

Number: 39	**Age Group:** Seven year olds
Date: November	**Number of players:** 24
Total time: 60 minutes	**Number of trainers:** 4
Location: Ice hockey Stadium	**Training aim:** Puck handling

Content of Training Unit

Beginning:
- Greeting, motivation.
- Catching game, stretching and breathing exercises.

Warm-up and Main part:
- "Rugby" with a ball – played as 6 x 2:2 (each group of 4 players have a ball).
  - Handle the ball as in "rugby".
  - After a fall, the player must give the ball up immediately.
- Puck handling – around the rink.
  - Alternate between short and long dribbling.
- Puck handling in curves – as groups between the goal line and the blue line.
- Puck handling – all the players in one game zone.
  - One sixth of the players have no puck.
  - On a signal, the players with the pucks leave these lying and, together with the players without a puck, try to get a fresh one.
- "Playing for the pucks": Puck handling on the whole rink. One of the players (without a puck) tries to touch the puck held by someone else. If he succeeds then the player affected has to continue without the puck.
- Backwards cross-over – the size of the circle alters gradually.
- Forwards cross-over – the size of the circle alters gradually, and on a signal skate in a curve (left, right).
- "Bringing the other players off balance": On a signal everyone skates a figure of eight.

TRAINING EXAMPLES

- Game with the pucks – diagonally in single playing zones. The goals have been turned round. A goal only counts when it is shot from behind (see Diagram 52).
- Play is done 2 x 2:2 (i.e., 2 play against 2 in each playing zone, each pair has a puck).

Conclusion:
- "Figure skating" freely around: Each trainer has his own group and demonstrates various tricks, which the players have to copy.
- Meeting, training assessment.

Notes:
- During the training unit, fit in stretching and breathing exercises.
- As required take time out between the individual exercises for a drink and a check of the equipment.

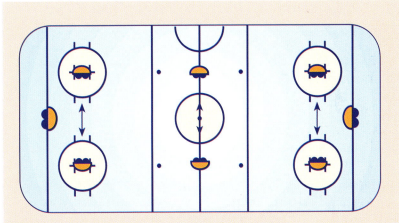

Diagram 52

HOCKEY
FIRST STEPS FOR KIDS

Number: 50	**Age Group:** Seven year olds
Date: December	**Number of players:** 60
Total time: 60 minutes	**Number of trainers:** 6
Location: Ice hockey Stadium	**Training aim:** Passing, shooting at goal

Content of Training Unit

Warm-up:
- Greeting, motivation.
- Game – "The Magician": In the center of the playing area, there is a "magician" standing with a magic wand. Whenever he holds his stick above his head, everyone has to skate to him with their knees bent. Whenever the stick falls back down on the ice, everyone has to go back into a circle. The magician follows them and whoever he catches is the next magician.
- Stretching exercises.

Main part:
- Exercises at five stations plus goalie training with a change round every 10 minutes. At each stand there is a trainer (assistant).

Stations/Stands
1) Mini hockey.
2) Ice-skating forwards and backwards.
3) Passing on the spot.
4) Passing when skating forwards.
5) Wrist shot at the side boards while standing still.

Conclusion:
- Ice-skating with the trainers in groups. The players copy what the trainers are doing.
- Breathing, loosening the muscles and stretching exercises.
- Meeting, training assessment.

TRAINING EXAMPLES

Notes:
- The players have already done a basic course in ice-skating.
- The training unit is conducted in stations, so that the children can be divided up into groups according to their individual skills.
- When changing stations, a time out should be allowed for to take a drink and check the equipment.

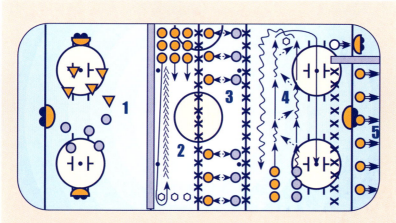

Diagram 53

HOCKEY
FIRST STEPS FOR KIDS

Number: 52	**Age Group:** Seven year olds
Date: November	**Number of players:** 25
Total time: 60 minutes	**Number of trainers:** 3
Location: Ice hockey Stadium	**Training aim:** Puck handling

Content of Training Unit

Beginning:
- Greeting, motivations.
- Game – The "eagle" and the "hawk": The players are divided up into two groups. In both nests (the face-off circles) there are a certain amount of pucks (eggs). On a signal both groups try to get as many eggs into their nest as possible. Body play is not allowed.

Warm-up and Main part:
- "Rugby" with a ball 4:4: Each four man group has a ball. All play on one playing area (shortened length) with two goals that have been turned round.
- Puck handling on the spot – cross the legs, short and long dribbling.
- Puck handling when doing the cross-over – round the face-off circle.
- "Playing for the pucks": Puck handling over the whole rink. One player, without a puck, tries to touch the puck of another player. If he is successful then the player hands over his puck and drops out. The game goes on until only one player is left with the puck.
- Backwards cross-over around the whole rink doing a snake.
- Backwards cross-over doing a figure of eight.
- Doing curves with forward cross-overs – do a 'stiff' slalom (see Diagram 54).
- Game 2:2: The play is done diagonally in a game zone. Each pair has a puck and plays against another pair. All the pairs, however, play against both goals (e.g., with 24 players two sets of 2 versus 2 pairs – total eight players – with two pucks in a single game zone) – a goal only counts when the goal has been skated around.

130

TRAINING EXAMPLES

Conclusion:
- Game: "The reds and the whites".
- Stretching and breathing exercises.

Notes:
- During the training unit, fit in stretching and breathing exercises.
- As required, a time out should be allowed for between exercises to take a drink and check the equipment.

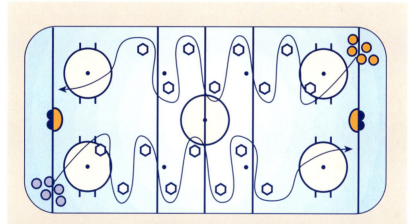

Diagram 54

HOCKEY
FIRST STEPS FOR KIDS

Number: 60	**Age Group:** Seven year olds
Date: January	**Number of players:** 30
Total time: 60 minutes	**Number of trainers:** 4
Location: Ice hockey Stadium	**Training aim:** Individual game skills, Ice-skating

Content of Training Unit

Beginning:
- Greeting, motivation.

Warm-up and Main part:
- "Soccer with balls" 4:4: At the same time 3 x 4:4 play with three balls. As they play they twirl the stick round the body.
- Puck handling – slalom (see Diagram 55a), do various dribbling versions.
- Puck handling – around cones (see Diagram 55b).
- Puck handling – in pairs, doing copy-cat. The first player dribbles the puck in different directions, the second player tries to copy him – do continuous cross-overs.
- Backwards cross-over – around the circle. On a signal do a turn backwards and outwards and continue crossing over in the other direction (see Diagram 56).
- Ice-skating forwards – down a slalom course, cross-over round a cone (see Diagram 57).
- Mini hockey – 4:4 in single game zones.

Conclusion:
- Game "The reds and the whites".
- Stretching and breathing exercises.
- Meeting, training assessment.

Notes:
- During the training unit, fit in stretching and breathing exercises.
- As required, a time out should be allowed for between exercises to take a drink and check the equipment.

TRAINING EXAMPLES

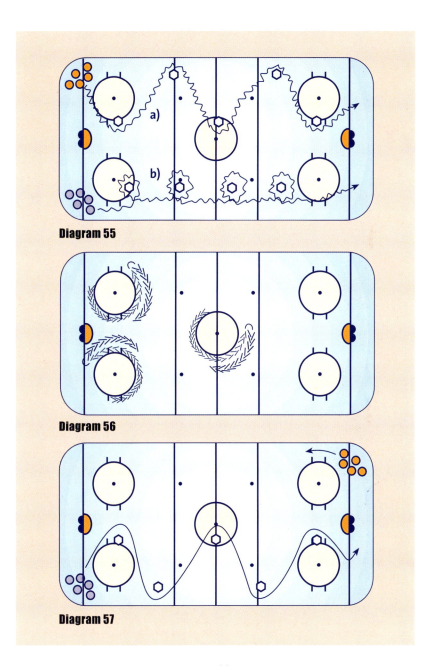

Diagram 55

Diagram 56

Diagram 57

HOCKEY
FIRST STEPS FOR KIDS

Number: 64	**Age Group:** Seven year olds
Date: February	**Number of players:** 60
Total time: 75 minutes	**Number of trainers:** 7
Location: Ice hockey Stadium	**Training aim:** Individual game skills, Ice-skating

Content of Training Unit

Warm-up:
- Meeting, training assessment.
- Any game.
- Stretching.

Main part:
- Exercises at six stations plus goalie training with a change round every 10 minutes. At each stand there is a trainer (assistant).

Stations/Stands
1) Wrist shot.
2) Ice-skating without a puck – forwards and backwards.
3) Ice-skating over obstacles.
4) Ice-skating forwards with cross-overs.
5) Puck handling in different directions.
6) Puck handling and shots at goal.

Conclusion:
- Little games.
- Stretching and breathing exercises.
- Meeting, training assessment.

Notes:
- The players have already done a basic course in ice-skating.

TRAINING EXAMPLES

- The training unit is conducted in stations, so that the children can be divided up into groups according to their individual skills.
- When changing stations, a time out should be allowed for to take a drink and check the equipment.

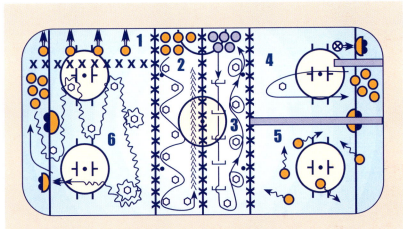

Diagram 58

HOCKEY
FIRST STEPS FOR KIDS

Number: 66	**Age Group:** Seven year olds
Date: February	**Number of players:** 22
Total time: 60 minutes	**Number of trainers:** 3
Location: Ice hockey Stadium	**Training aim:** Individual game skills, Ice-skating

Content of Training Unit

Beginning:
■ Greeting, motivation.
■ Stretching on the spot.

Warm-up and Main part
■ "Tripping" – 1:1.
■ Puck handling – slalom, (the longer the course the tighter the cones are together).
■ Puck handling – in figures of eight (between two cones).
■ Puck handling – Catching game 1:1 on the whole of the rink. On a signal, all do a circuit of cross-overs round the next face-off circle.
■ Backwards cross-over – round the face-off circle. On a signal all do a circuit in the opposite direction (see Diagram 59a).
■ Forwards cross-over – round the face-off circle. On a signal skate a curve and do a little circuit outwards, changing over from outside to inside (see Diagram 59b).
■ Game with the puck – 2:2. Done on a shortened area of the rink, 5 x 2:2 against two goals, at the same time 5 pucks are in play.

Conclusion:
■ Little games.
■ Stretching and breathing exercises.
■ Meeting, training assessment.

TRAINING EXAMPLES

Notes:
- During the training unit, fit in stretching and breathing exercises.
- As required, a time out should be allowed for between exercises to take a drink and check the equipment.

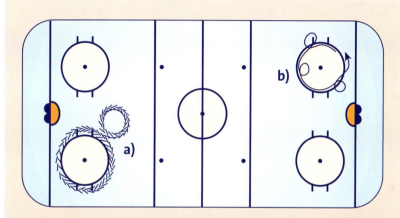

Diagram 59

HOCKEY
FIRST STEPS FOR KIDS

Number: 72	**Age Group:** Seven year olds
Date: March	**Number of players:** 24
Total time: 60 minutes	**Number of trainers:** 3
Location: Ice hockey Stadium	**Training aim:** Individual game skills, Ice-skating

Content of Training Unit

Beginning:
- Greeting, motivation.
- Stretching exercises on the spot.

Warm-up and Main part:
- Catching game – "the Ram": The player being caught skates forwards, the others skate backwards. The Ram can only touch the player being caught on the head. Whoever is caught this way joins in with the "Ram".
- Puck handling – slalom (the cones are placed about 6 m from each other – see Diagram 60a).
- Practicing the simple evading maneuver with the aid of the cones – the fake out should be practiced from the beginning (see Diagram 60b).
- Puck handling in pairs: The one player copies the other, each player has a puck.
- Backwards cross-overs round the face-off circle: On a signal, alternately, do a little circuit to the outside and then the inside (see Training Unit No 66).
- Catching game: 1:1 while skating backwards. The catch is made using the stick.
- Game on a shortened playing area: At the same time 3 x 4:4 players (according to the total number of players present) with 3 pucks (each 4:4 group have a puck).

Conclusion:
- Little games.
- Stretching and breathing exercises.
- Meeting, training assessment.

TRAINING EXAMPLES

Notes:
- During the training unit, fit in stretching and breathing exercises.
- As required, a time out should be allowed for between exercises to take a drink and check the equipment.

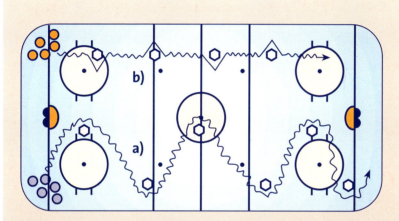

Diagram 60

TRAINING EXAMPLES FOR AN EIGHT YEAR OLD

Number: 8

Date: August

Total time: 60 minutes

Location: Ice hockey Stadium

Age Group: Eight year olds

Number of players: 30

Number of trainers: 3

Training aim: Individual game skills, ice-skating

Content of Training Unit

Beginning:
- Greeting, motivation.
- Free skating with the trainer.
- Stretching exercises on the spot.

Warm-up and Main part:
- Catching game – "the Ram": The player being caught skates forwards, the others skate backwards. The Ram can only touch the player being caught on the head. Whoever is caught this way joins in with the "Ram".
- Braking and push-off start in the opposite direction (see Diagram 61).
- Turning – from a forwards into a backwards skating direction, and from a backwards into a forwards skating direction (see Diagram 61).
- Doing the cross-over forwards and backwards – skating a spiral figure doing one turn each time (see Diagram 62).
- Passing from a standing position with the players standing opposite.
- Puck handling and passes on the move (see Diagram 63).
- Game in one of the game zones: 2:2 play diagonally at the same time (altogether 6 x 2:2) with a puck in a game zone and they all play against the same two goals.
- Game – The "man in the middle": The player in the middle of the face-off circle tries to get the puck. If he succeeds then the players change over. Played in all of the face-off circles.

TRAINING EXAMPLES

Conclusion:
- Stretching and breathing exercises.
- Meeting, training assessment.

Notes:
- During the training unit, fit in stretching and breathing exercises.
- As required, a time out should be allowed for between exercises to take a drink and check the equipment.

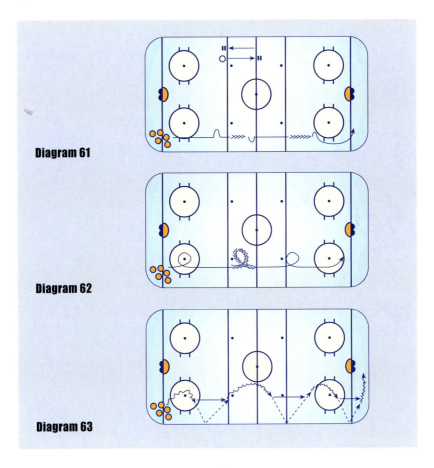

Diagram 61

Diagram 62

Diagram 63

HOCKEY
FIRST STEPS FOR KIDS

Number: 12	**Age Group:** Eight year olds
Date: September	**Number of players:** 25
Total time: 75 minutes	**Number of trainers:** 3
Location: Ice hockey Stadium	**Training aim:** Individual game skills, ice-skating

Content of Training Unit

Beginning:
- Greeting, motivation.
- Free skating with the trainers.
- Stretching exercises.

Warm-up and Main part:
- Catching game – 1:1: Skating forwards touching hands. On a signal carry out a full turn and both skate backwards with sticks touching, on a signal turn again etc.
- Braking and push-off starts – after turning on the spot (see Diagram 64).
- Turn training – on the move, going around to the left skating backwards and then immediately go right in a turn and skate forwards, then go straight (see Diagram 65a) and into a spiral turn (see Diagram 65b).
- Taking shots at the side-boards – moving slowly, using the wrist shot.
- Puck handling after the pass. The puck is received frontally, after the turn and the cross-over (see Diagram 66a).
- Puck handling and a shot at goal – wrist shot (see Diagram 66b).
- Game: Mini hockey in the single game zones (4:4).

Conclusion:
- Stretching and breathing exercises.
- Meeting, training assessment.

Notes:
- During the training unit, fit in stretching and breathing exercises.

TRAINING EXAMPLES

■ As required, a time out should be allowed for between exercises to take a drink and check the equipment.

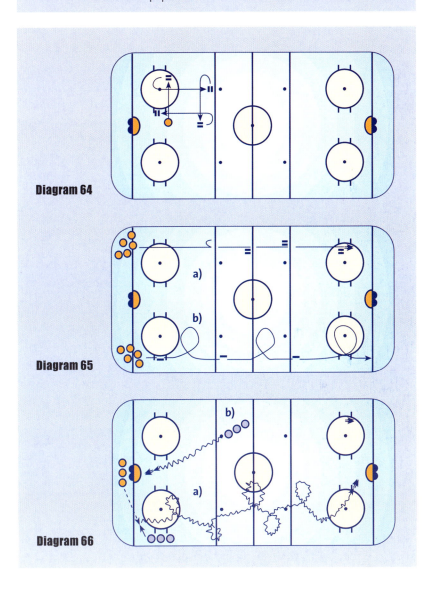

Diagram 64

Diagram 65

Diagram 66

HOCKEY
FIRST STEPS FOR KIDS

Number: 14

Date: September

Total time: 90 minutes

Location: Ice hockey Stadium

Age Group: Eight year olds

Number of players: 40

Number of trainers: 7

Training aim: Individual game skills, ice-skating

Content of Training Unit

Beginning:
- Greeting, motivation.
- Any game.
- Stretching exercises.

Warm up and Main part:
- Exercises at seven stations with a change round every 10 minutes. At each stand there is a trainer (assistant).

Stations/Stands
1) Puck handling and wrist shot.
2) Puck handling- forwards and backwards.
3) Puck handling (cross-overs, skating curves) and ending up with a shot.
4) 1:1 – Tackling for the puck, evading maneuvers.
5) Puck handling in different directions.
6) Passing on the move, practiced in pairs.
7) Puck handling and wrist shots at goal.

Conclusion:
- Mini hockey in single game zones.
- Breathing, loosening the muscles and stretching exercises.
- Meeting, training assessment.

Notes:
- The players have already done a basic course in ice-skating.

TRAINING EXAMPLES

- The training unit is conducted in stations, so that the children can be divided up into groups according to their individual skills.
- When changing stations, a time out should be allowed for to take a drink and check the equipment.

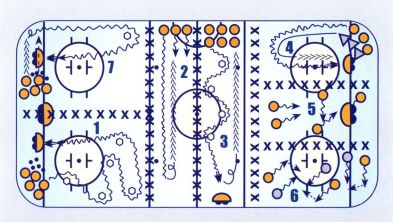

Diagram 67

HOCKEY
FIRST STEPS FOR KIDS

Number: 26	**Age Group:** Eight year olds
Date: October	**Number of players:** 25
Total time: 75 minutes	**Number of trainers:** 3
Location: Ice hockey Stadium	**Training aim:** Individual game skills, ice-skating

Content of Training Unit

Beginning:
- Greeting, motivation.
- Game.
- Stretching exercises.

Warm-up and Main part:
- Game – "Deep frozen": In a game zone, everyone skates forwards. On a signal they all turn into a backwards skating motion. They can save themselves by skating underneath the bridge – arm holding out the stick (see Diagram 46 in Training Unit No 53).
- Stopping when skating backwards (see Diagram 68a).
- Full turns – from forwards into a turn and forwards again. From backwards again into backwards after a full turn.
- Long evading maneuver (see Diagram 68b).
- Passing on the move – in pairs (see Diagram 69). The pass and the receipt are done sideways on to the puck.
- Puck handling in a slalom course – faster: In pairs, the player without the puck turns round on a signal and skates after the partner in puck possession, who has to finish off the exercise with a shot at goal (see Diagram 70).
- Game on the whole rink – (a shortened version is also possible). During the game, player substitution is done without a break in play.

Conclusion:
- Game: The " man in the middle" stands in a face-off circle. After a pass each player turns round 360º.

TRAINING EXAMPLES

- Breathing, loosening the muscles and stretching exercises.
- Meeting, training assessment.

Notes:
- During the training unit, fit in stretching and breathing exercises.
- As required, a time out should be allowed for between exercises to take a drink and check the equipment.

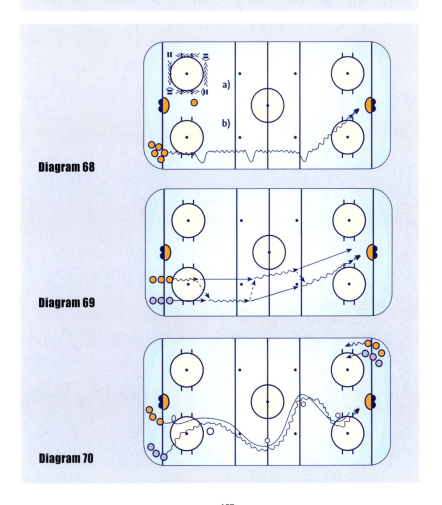

Diagram 68

Diagram 69

Diagram 70

HOCKEY
FIRST STEPS FOR KIDS

Number: 38	**Age Group:** Eight year olds
Date: November	**Number of players:** 25
Total time: 70 minutes	**Number of trainers:** 3
Location: Ice hockey Stadium	**Training aim:** Individual game skills, ice-skating

Content of Training Unit

Beginning:
- Greeting, motivation.
- Little games
- Stretching exercises.

Warm-up and Main part:
- Catching game 1:1: While skating forwards, a signal is given and all turn round 360º.
- Turning: By doing the forwards cross-over into a backwards cross-over movement and vice versa.
- "Flying turn": Doing a turn from skating forwards into skating backwards and then immediately back into skating forwards doing cross-overs.
- Doing figures of eight with turns.
- Puck handling: Do a long evading maneuver round cones and finish off with a wrist shot at goal (see Diagram 71).
- Puck handling: After a pass, try to catch a partner through a tight slalom. The player passing turns round and follows the player with the puck, who finishes off the exercise with a shot at goal (see Diagram 72).
- Game: Shortened rink length with four goals. 2 x 4:4 play at the same time. Goals count after a shot in one of the opponent's goals (there are two goals) (see Diagram 73).

Conclusion:
- Free puck handling: The players carry out a long evading maneuver against an imaginary opponent and finish off with a shot at goal (skating round the playing area).

TRAINING EXAMPLES

- Breathing, loosening the muscles and stretching exercises.
- Meeting, training assessment.

Notes:
- During the training unit, fit in stretching and breathing exercises.
- As required, a time out should be allowed for between exercises to take a drink and check the equipment.

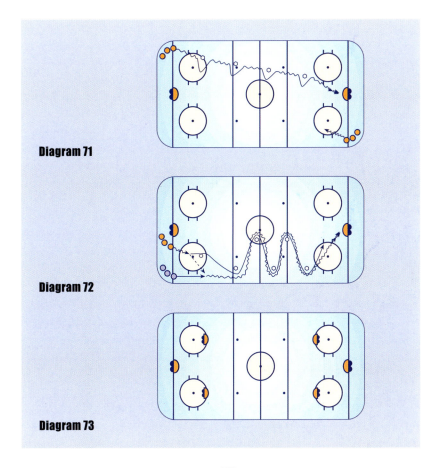

Diagram 71

Diagram 72

Diagram 73

149

HOCKEY
FIRST STEPS FOR KIDS

Number: 40	**Age Group:** Eight year olds
Date: November	**Number of players:** 40
Total time: 60 minutes	**Number of trainers:** 5
Location: Ice hockey Stadium	**Training aim:** Individual game skills, ice-skating

Content of Training Unit

Beginning:
- Greeting, motivation.
- Little games.
- Stretching exercises.

Warm-up and Main part:
- Exercises at four stations with a change round every 10 minutes. At each stand there is a trainer (assistant) and goalkeeper instructor.

Stations/Stands
1) Mini hockey.
2) Skating backwards – tricks – turning, kneeling, braking etc.
3) Skating backwards without the puck and doing puck handling through a slalom course, ending up with a wrist shot.
4) Puck handling through a slalom course and doing a shot off the move.
5) Goal-keeping practice.

Conclusion:
- 10 minutes doing different little games with emphasis on ice-skating..
- Breathing, loosening the muscles and stretching exercises.
- Meeting, training assessment.

Notes:
- The players have already done a basic course in ice-skating.

TRAINING EXAMPLES

- The training unit is conducted in stations, so that the children can be divided up into groups according to their individual skills.
- When changing stations, a time out should be allowed for to take a drink and check the equipment.

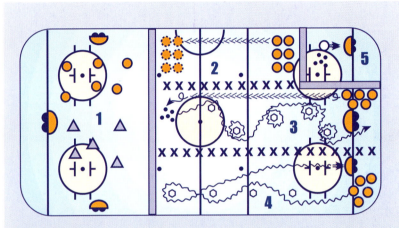

Diagram 74

HOCKEY
FIRST STEPS FOR KIDS

Number: 52	**Age Group:** Eight year olds
Date: December	**Number of players:** 25
Total time: 60 minutes	**Number of trainers:** 3
Location: Ice hockey Stadium	**Training aim:** Individual game skills, ice-skating

Content of Training Unit

Beginning:
- Greeting, motivation.
- Skating freely with the trainer in groups.
- Stretching exercises.

Warm-up and Main part:
- Game – "Deep frozen": Everyone skates forwards. They can save themselves by skating underneath the bridge – arm holding out the stick. After the turn they do a backwards skating motion and then go back into skating forwards.
- Full turns – from forwards cross-over. When doing the cross-over to the left the turn is done round to the right and in the opposite direction (see Diagram 75a).
- Doing figures of eight with half turns out of skating forwards into skating backwards and from backwards into forwards with a full turn in the middle (see Diagram 75b)
- Puck handling: Doing cross-overs quickly round the cones as a catching game 1:1. The player being chased does a turn after he starts, and on the blue line he stops still and frees the defending player. The player with the puck does an evading maneuver and finishes off the exercise with a wrist shot at goal (see Diagram 76).
- Game in a game zone – 5 x (6 x) 2:2 play at the same time against goals, which have been turned round. Goals can be scored only from behind (see Diagram 77).

TRAINING EXAMPLES

Conclusion:
- Game: The "man in the middle" stands in a face-off circle. After a pass the player takes three steps, brakes and comes back..
- Stretching and breathing exercises.
- Meeting, training assessment.

Notes:
- During the training unit, fit in stretching and breathing exercises.
- As required, a time out should be allowed for between exercises to take a drink and check the equipment.

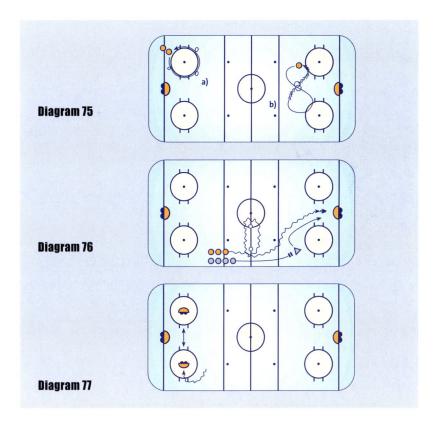

Diagram 75

Diagram 76

Diagram 77

HOCKEY
FIRST STEPS FOR KIDS

Number: 58	**Age Group:** Eight year olds
Date: January	**Number of players:** 25
Total time: 75 minutes	**Number of trainers:** 3
Location: Ice hockey Stadium	**Training aim:** Individual game skills, ice-skating

Content of Training Unit

Beginning:
- Greeting, motivation.
- Little games
- Stretching exercises.

Warm-up and Main part:
- "Bringing the other players off balance": On a signal all skate forwards and skate round the rink. Then they skate backwards and then turn again into skating forwards.
- Skating through a slalom: On the one side of the rink do turns, forwards cross-overs, skating backwards and forwards (see Diagram 78a). On the other side of the rink do "flying half turns", turning with a cross-over forwards (see Diagram 78b).
- Evading maneuver with fake outs plus a long evading maneuver across the rink (see Diagram 79a).
- Feinting an evading maneuver against cones – the slalom gets tighter (see Diagram 79b).
- Puck handling with a feinting evading maneuver. After the pass, the puck is moved on, followed by an evading maneuver against a player standing, who after the maneuver follows the player in possession. The player who is doing the pass, starts, does a full turn and takes the place of the defending player (see Diagram 80).
- Game: Mini hockey in single game zones 4:4.

154

TRAINING EXAMPLES

Conclusion:
- Free puck handling around the rink, feinting evading maneuvers, and attack on the goalie with a fake out.
- Stretching and breathing exercises.
- Meeting, training assessment.

Notes:
- During the training unit, fit in stretching and breathing exercises.
- As required, a time out should be allowed for between exercises to take a drink and check the equipment.

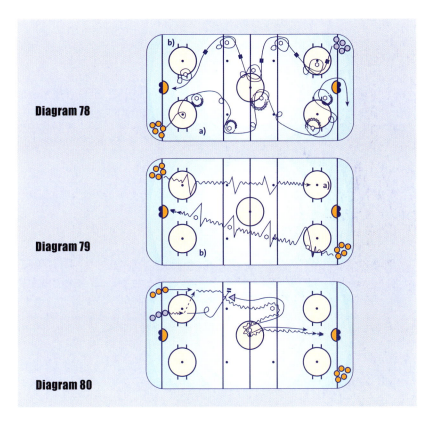

Diagram 78

Diagram 79

Diagram 80

HOCKEY
FIRST STEPS FOR KIDS

Number: 64	**Age Group:** Eight year olds
Date: February	**Number of players:** 25
Total time: 60 minutes	**Number of trainers:** 3
Location: Ice hockey Stadium	**Training aim:** Individual game skills, ice-skating

Content of Training Unit

Beginning:
- Greeting, motivation.
- Skating freely in groups with the trainer.
- Stretching exercises.

Warm-up and Main part:
- Catching game 1:1 in a circle: 3 pairs (3 x 1:1) play in a circle skating forwards. Catching is only by touching the head. Players continually are doing feinting maneuvers with frequent, rapid changes of direction.
- Do forward cross-overs round the face-off circle – when doing the cross-over to the left a full turn to the right is done, followed by a curve and then cross-overs (see Diagram 81a).
- Half and full turns: Do half turns on the fly to the left and back again; whole turns to the right (see Diagram 81b). Speed and frequency are important.
- Puck handling with an evading maneuver – on one side of the rink do evading maneuvers towards the outside in a slalom (see Diagram 82a). On the other side of the rink do an evading maneuver to the inside around the slalom (see Diagram 82b).
- Puck handling with a catching game after a pass (see Diagram 83). The player takes the puck on, feints a movement and makes an evading maneuver against the player opposite on the blue line and then shoots. The player who has done the pass does a turn and takes the place of the defender. He then follows the player in possession of the puck in the neutral zone. On the second blue line he takes up the position of the

TRAINING EXAMPLES

defending player, and the player who has been defending up until now, follows the player in possession until he shoots at the end of the exercise.
- Game – on the whole playing area 5:5. Substitution occurs without a break in play (after about 30 seconds).

Conclusion:
- Game – "the man in the middle": Five players stand round the face-off circle. Each player skates in the direction of the pass.
- Stretching and breathing exercises.
- Meeting, training assessment.

Notes:
- During the training unit, fit in stretching and breathing exercises.
- As required, a time out should be allowed for between exercises to take a drink and check the equipment.

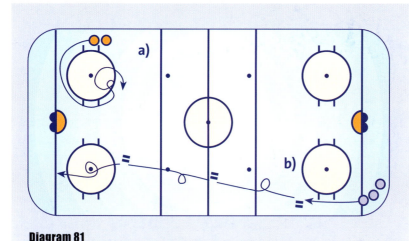

Diagram 81

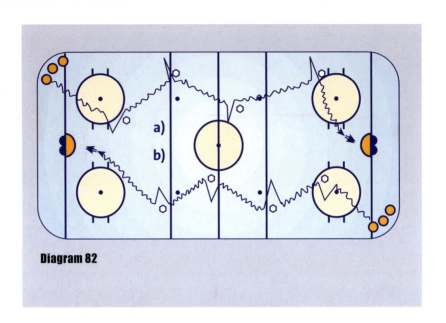

Diagram 82

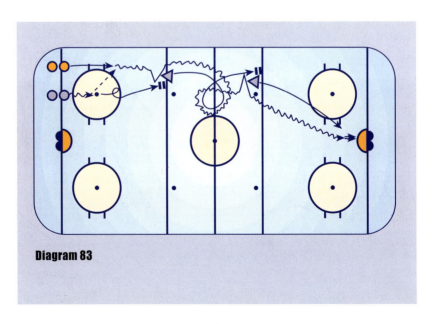

Diagram 83

TRAINING EXAMPLES

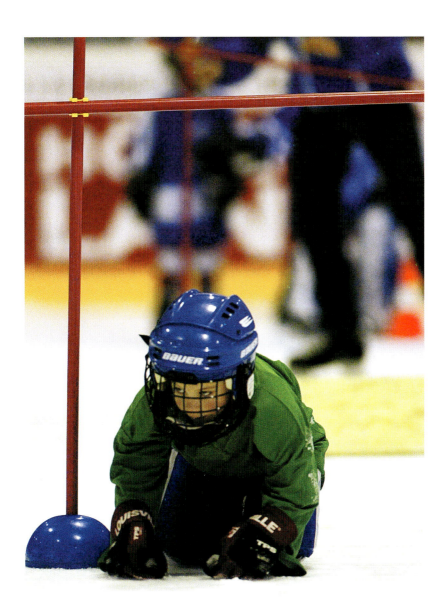

HOCKEY
FIRST STEPS FOR KIDS

Number: 66	**Age Group:** Eight year olds
Date: February	**Number of players:** 40
Total time: 75 minutes	**Number of trainers:** 4
Location: Ice hockey Stadium	**Training aim:** Individual game skills, ice-skating

Content of Training Unit

Beginning:
- Greeting, motivation.
- Little games.
- Stretching exercises.

Warm-up and Main part:
- Exercises at four stations with a change round every 15 minutes. At each stand there is a trainer (assistant) and goalkeeper instructor.

Stations/Stands
1) Evading maneuvers ending up with a shot at goal.
2) Situation 1:1- for the attacking forward emphasis on evading maneuvers; for the defender emphasis at tackling the puck away.
3) In pairs – passing and shooting.
4) Puck handling, passing off the side-boards, slalom course and shooting on the move.

Conclusion:
- 15 minutes doing mini hockey in single game zones.
- Breathing, loosening the muscles and stretching exercises.
- Meeting, training assessment.

Notes:
- The players have already done a basic course in ice-skating.
- The training unit is conducted in stations, so that the children can be divided up into groups according to their individual skills.

160

TRAINING EXAMPLES

- When changing stations, a time out should be allowed for to take a drink and check the equipment.

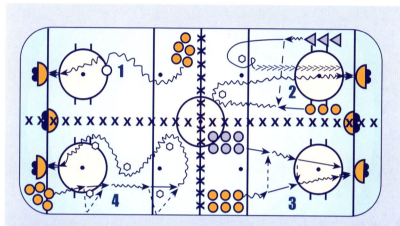

Diagram 84

HOCKEY
FIRST STEPS FOR KIDS

Number: 71	**Age Group:** Eight year olds
Date: March	**Number of players:** 25
Total time: 60 minutes	**Number of trainers:** 4
Location: Ice hockey Stadium	**Training aim:** Individual game skills, ice-skating

Content of Training Unit

Beginning:
- Greeting, motivation.
- Game.
- Stretching exercises.

Warm-up and Main part:
- "Deep frozen": all skate forwards, the captured player lies down. He can be saved by someone jumping over him.
- Cross-over to the left: Do a half turn to the left skating forwards and then a curve with the cross-over. Do a half turn skating backwards, backward cross-over to the left (see Diagram 85).
- Trick skating: Skating forwards with the cross-over, flying half turn to the left, turn to the right, half a turn, turn, stop, start off forwards, skate backwards, half a turn to the left, cross-over to the left etc (see Diagram 86).
- Game – the "spoiler" in the face-off circle: After passing do a full turn.
- Puck handling being chased (see Diagram 87): Puck handling after the pass, feinting and evading maneuver against the defending (standing) player, on the red line skate in a curve and do a cross-over to the left, do another curve and cross-over to the right, on the blue line in the attacking zone do the same and finish off with a shot at goal. The player who passed the puck turns round and takes up the place of the defending player. He follows the player in possession and does turns.
- Game: Done on a shortened playing area, 4:4 – player substitution without a break in play.

162

TRAINING EXAMPLES

Conclusion:
- Free puck handling with shooting practice, feinting and turns etc.
- Breathing, loosening the muscles and stretching exercises.
- Meeting, training assessment.

Notes:
- During the training unit, fit in stretching and breathing exercises.
- As required, a time out should be allowed for between exercises to take a drink and check the equipment.

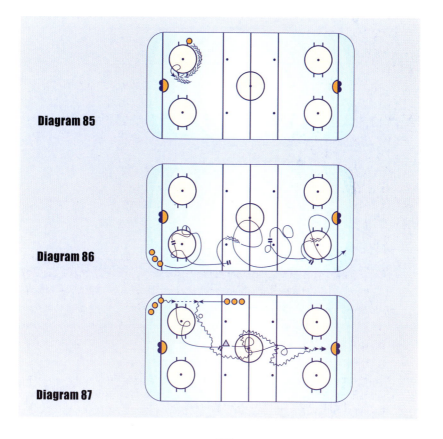

Diagram 85

Diagram 86

Diagram 87

HOCKEY
FIRST STEPS FOR KIDS

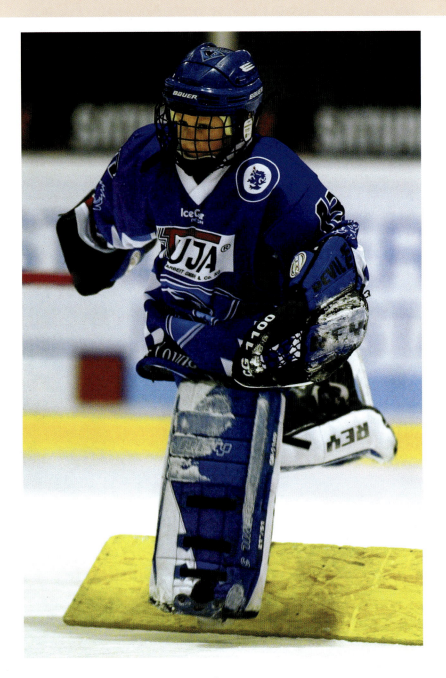

EXERCISES

Skating with the Puck and the Stick

Exercise 1
The player skates in a zigzag line and dribbles short (faking). The exercise is finished off with a shot at goal.

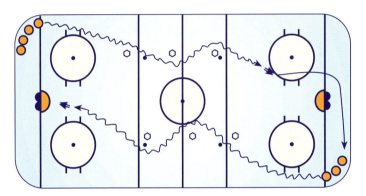

Exercise 2
Slalom courses are done in the single game zones together with various dribbling and shooting versions.

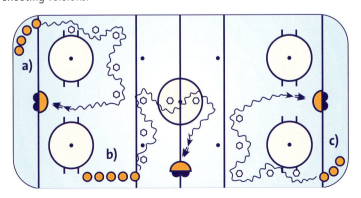

Exercise 3
Various slalom versions done in a game zone. The emphasis is on faking and the correct puck handling technique.

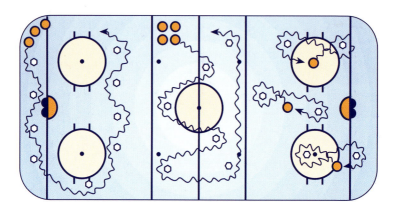

Exercise 4
a) Straight puck driving (diagonally to the game zone). Do a drop pass to another player.
b)+c) Puck handling with the cross-over.
d) Puck handling in the slalom course, on the return route skate backwards.

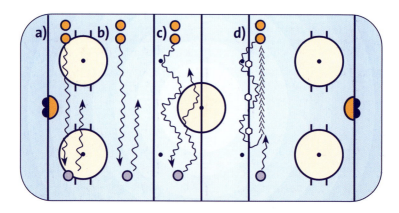

Exercise 5
a) Do a slalom course in one of the game zones, shoot at the boards.
b) Puck handling in different directions inside a game zone.

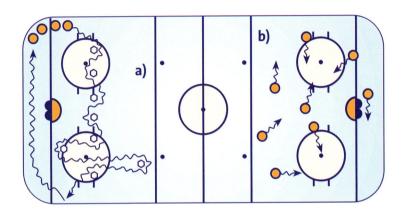

Exercise 6
Different versions of puck handling – diagonally in the game zone.

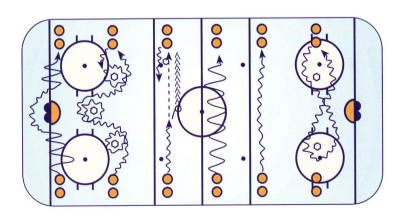

Exercise 7

The players form a square and dribble the puck in different directions.

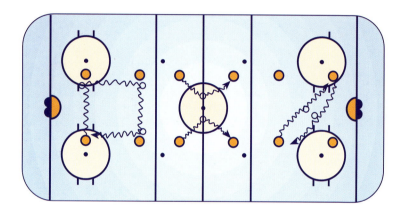

Exercise 8

a) The players dribble a puck through a slalom course, faking round the cones and the exercise finishes with a shot at the end boards.
b) The players dribble a puck through a slalom course, in order to evade the cones, they do a shot at the boards, while the player goes round the cone on the other side.

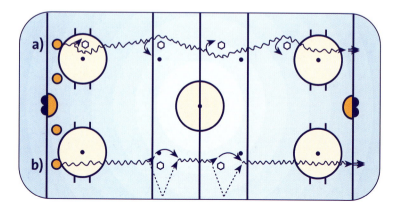

EXERCISES

Exercise 9
a) Puck dribbling round a teammate and a pass.
b) The players form squares and attack each other.
c) Doing a slalom skating backwards, with a shot at goal.

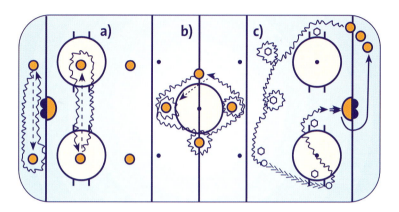

Exercise 10
a) Puck handling round the face-off circle and stopping.
b) Puck handling round the face-off circle skating forwards and backwards.
c) Puck handling in the game zone (diagonally).
d) Relay race – using different versions of puck handling.

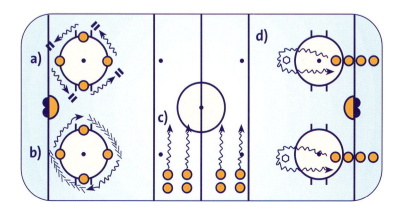

Exercise 11
Puck handling in a slalom followed by a turn, kneel down on one knee, shoot at goal.

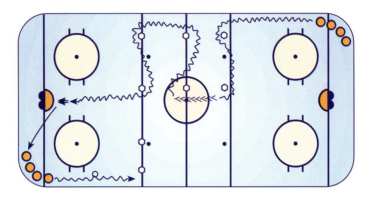

Exercise 12
The players stand opposite each other along the side-boards.
a) Skate round the cones with faking.
b) Skating round the cones.
c) Faking and turning.
d) Faking against a opponent and pass.
e) Turning against an opponent.

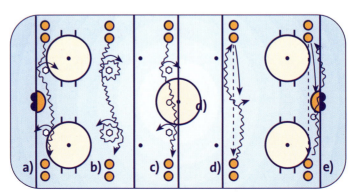

Passing and Receiving a Pass

Exercise 13
Passing – different forehand and backhand version, turns.

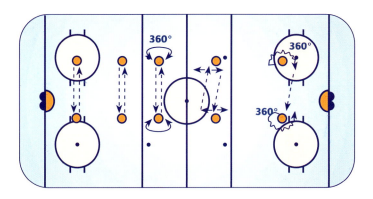

Exercise 14
"Passing and skating" (the player skates off immediately after making the pass) – with the player in different positions.

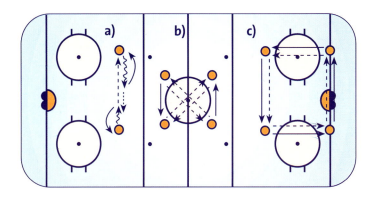

Exercise 15
a) "Passing and skating" – "Concertina".
b) The players are standing opposite each other, puck handling is done sideways, do passes and receive passes.
c) "Passing and skating" – Finish off: Shot at goal.

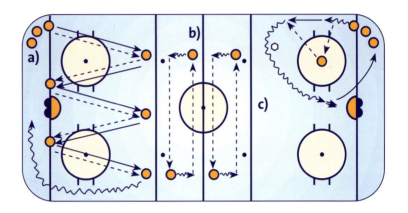

Exercise 16
In pairs – passes between the cones with a shot at goal to finish off.

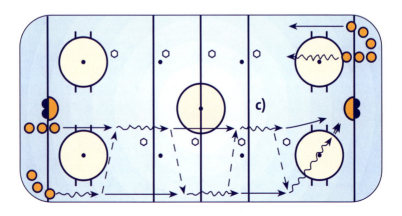

Exercise 17
a) In twos – the players are standing 5 m apart, passing on the move.
b) Passing to the other team – start.

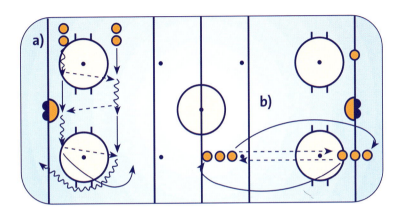

Exercise 18
2 x "passing and skating", skating round the cones on the red line and then a shot at goal.

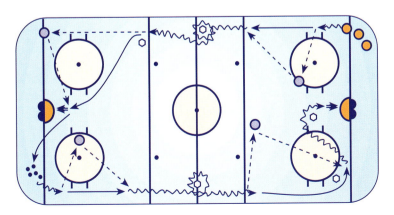

Exercise 19
a) Different passing versions in twos, skating forwards and backwards.
b) Passing game in twos on the move.
c) High passes above stick height.

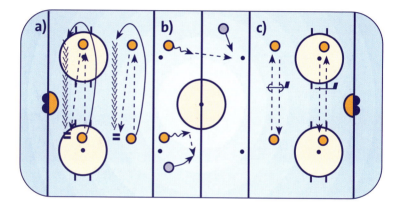

Exercise 20
In twos – passing on the move, with cross-overs.

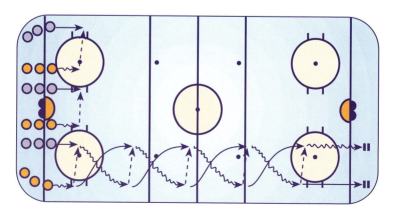

Exercise 21

a) In pairs – the one player in possession skates off, plays the puck to the other player who is skating backwards. A series of passes between them follows with both players alternating skating direction.
b) The player in possession of the puck skates off and plays the puck to the other player, using a turn he skates backwards and the takes a pass from the other player who has done the same thing as before.
c) Forehand and backhand passing in a sideways direction.

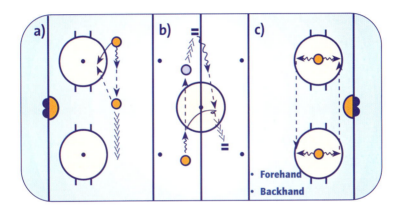

Shooting Training

Exercise 22

Shooting at the boards – using the correct technique for the wrist shot – emphasis – lifting the puck up.

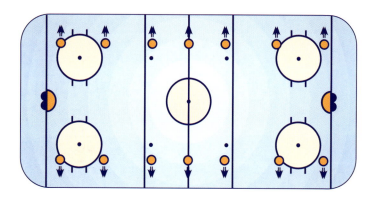

Exercise 23

Wrist shot at the boards on the move.

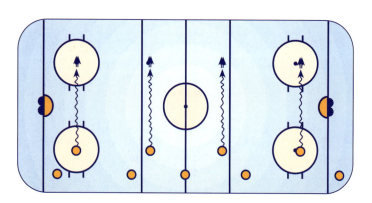

EXERCISES

Exercise 24
a) Wrist shot at goal, each player shoots 3 times one after the other.
b) Shots from a standing position into the boards – correct technique.
c) Shots in to the boards on the move.
d) Shots after a pass to a standing player.
e) Shots after pass while on the move.

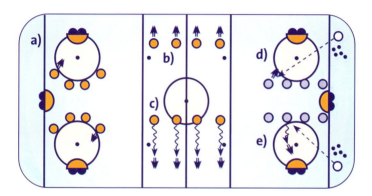

Exercise 25
a) Puck handling, bend the knees, kneel down, shot at goal.
b) Ice-skating without the puck, turn, kneel down, bend the knees – jump up, take a shot after receiving the puck.

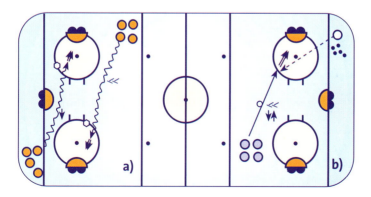

Exercise 26
Puck handling with tricks, shots at goal.

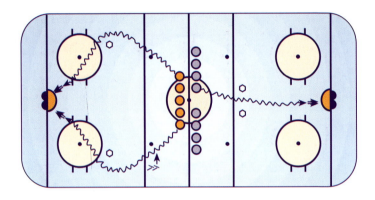

Exercise 27
a) Puck handling in the game zone round the face-off circle, wrist shot into the upper corner of the goal.
b) Puck handling with tricks, fake-out the cones, immediately do a wrsit shot at the upper corner of the goal.

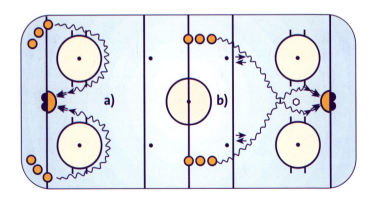

Exercise 28
Puck handling sideways, forehand and backhand shots into the boards.

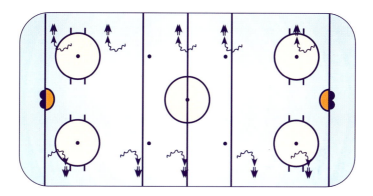

Exercise 29
a) "Passing and skating" accelerating, after receiving the puck a quick shot is made at goal. Following this the player collects the puck from the corner and rejoins his team.
b) The player skates round the cone and at the next one he does faking, shoots quickly at goal and fetches the puck out of the corner.

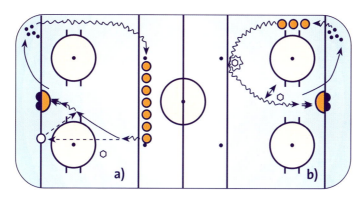

Exercise 30
a) Tricks without the puck, taking quick shots after receiving the puck, start in the corner.
b) Skate backwards without the puck, turn, receive the puck from a cross pass, fake-out round the cone and do a quick shot and skate on.

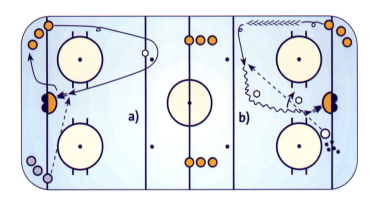

Exercise 31
a) Puck handling, skate round the cone, "passing and skating", after receiving the puck do tricks, then take a shot at goal.
b) Puck handling on a slalom course, evade round the cones, when doing the fake-out the puck is played off the boards and the take a shot at goal.

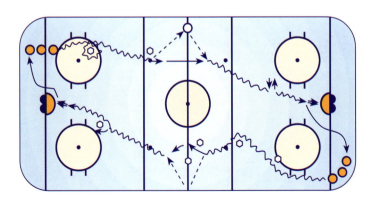

Exercise 32
The players are in single game zones:
a) Skating without the puck – various versions.
b) Passing on the move in pairs.
c) Shooting from a standing position – 3 pucks, shooting on the move.

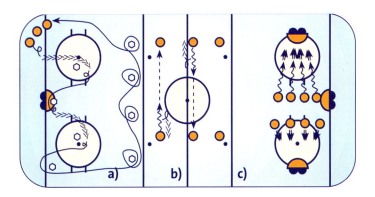

Exercise 33
a) Make a pass, do tricks without the puck, receive the puck and fake-out round a cone, do a shot.
b) Similar exercises in various versions.

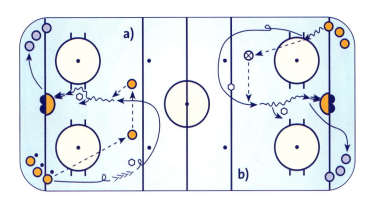

Receiving the Puck

Exercise 34
The defenders remain still, the attacking forwards skate up and practice different versions of tackling the puck away.

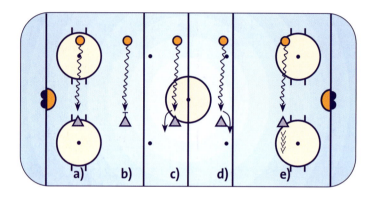

Exercise 35
Tackling the puck away on the boards; it is important when doing this to stand against the other player properly.

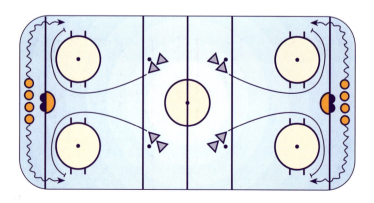

EXERCISES

Exercise 36
a) Skating up to the opponent, when he has gone behind his own goal.
b) Marking the opponent after a faking movement.

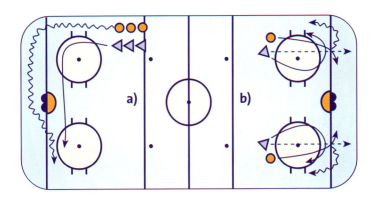

Exercise 37
a) Marking the opponent in possession of the puck in the corner.
Tackling the puck away after:
b) An evading movement and faking.
c) Playing through.

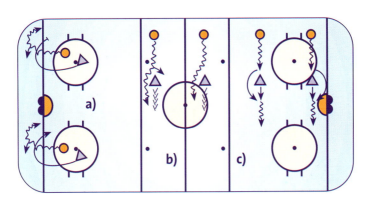

Exercise 38

The defending players are in the neutral playing zone, other players try to get through in possession of the puck – the emphasis is in tackling the puck away.

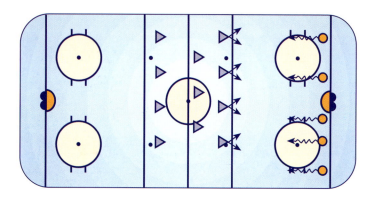

Exercise 39

a) Take up contact with the opponent in possession by skating forwards and doing a turn.
b) Take up contact with the opponent in possession by turning into a backwards skating motion followed by a turn.

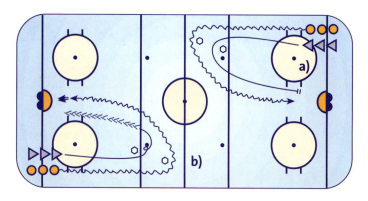

Exercise 40

a) Two players are against each other, each has a puck. The aim is to take the puck off the opponent without losing one's own. The players form up in a square while the defending player is in the middle.
b) The players skate alternately and diagonally, the defenders try to take the puck away using various different techniques.
c) One player to make a break-out after receiving a pass, the defender has to get the puck off him.

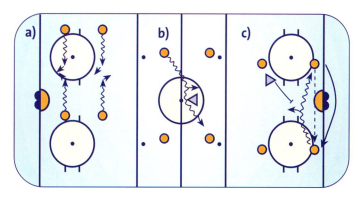

Exercise 41

The player in possession moves in different directions while the defender reacts accordingly.

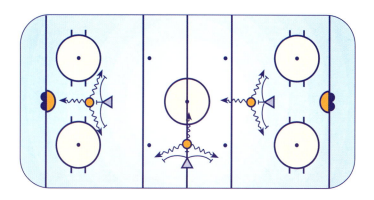

Exercise 42

A couple are moving around in the face-off circle and tackling each other for the puck (emphasis is on taking the puck away). A change takes place after the puck has been successfully won or one of the players leaves the circle.

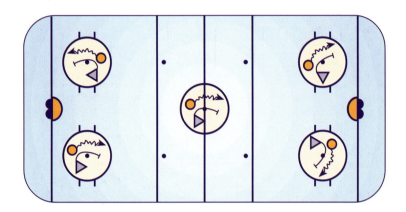

Exercise 43

The attacking player is attacked by a defender after receiving a pass from the trainer. If the defender gains possession of the puck, he gives it back to the trainer.

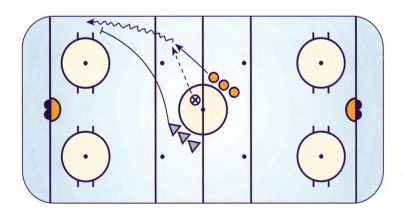

EXERCISES

Exercise 44
The player in possession of the puck skates through a pathway of defenders, who stay where they are and defend.

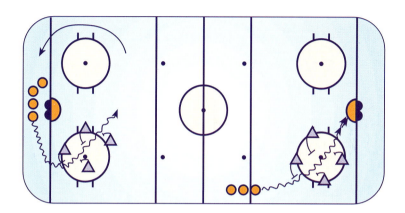

Exercise 45
A 1:1 situation takes place after a pass in the area surrounded by cones.

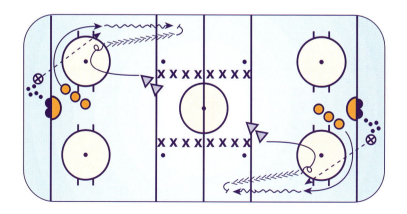

Exercise 46

The player in possession of the puck skates in to a good position to take a shot, where he is attacked by a defender. Important here are the correct direction of approach and the defender's efforts against the attacking forward.

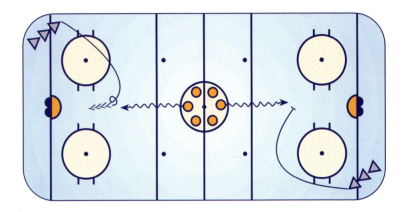

Exercise 47

2:2, fight to get the puck with the emphasis on marking the man.

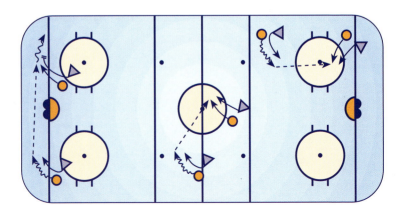

Exercise 48

The player without the puck skates into the corner of the attacking zone, receives a pass from a defender, who reacts to his movement. The attacking forward comes directly into the front of the goal or round behind it.

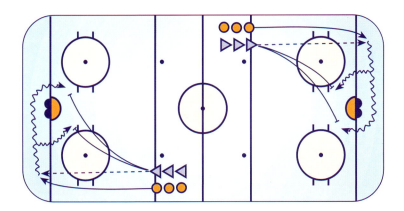

HOCKEY
FIRST STEPS FOR KIDS

APPENDICES

16 SYMBOLS

⊗	Trainer
●	Attacking player
▲	Defending player
⟶	Skating forwards not in puck possession
⫷⫷⫷	Skating backwards
⟶‖	Stopping
⫷	Kneeling
↓	Doing a knees bend
↑	Jumping up
∿∿⟶	Skating forwards in puck possession
- - - ⟶	Passing
⟴	Shooting
⊢	Attacking
⟝	Covering/protecting (the puck)
∴∵	Pucks
⬡	Training equipment and aids (cones/stands)
▭	Ice hockey stick

191

LITERATURE

Belmonte, Val. (1995): *Associaste Level Manual. Individual skill techniques. Handbook I, II.* USA Hockey.

Bukač, L. & Dovalíl, J. (1990): *Ledni hokej. Trénink herni dokonalosti.* Prag, Olympia.

Horáček, J. (1990): *Ledni hokej. Trenink.* Prag, Metodicky dopis CSLH.

Kostka, V. (1984): *Moderni hokej.* Prag, Olympia.

Lener, S. (1991): *Trenink švédských hokejistů.* Prag, Metodicky dopis CSLH.

Lener, S. (1983): *Celorocni program sportovni přípravy žactva v oddilech TJ. Ledni hokej.* Prag, Metodický dopis CUV CSTV.

Patterson, C. & Miller, J. (1990): *Initiation program. Lesson Manual A-D.* Ontario, CAHA Resource Centre.

Pavliš, Z. & Peric, T. (1996): *Abeceda hokejového brusleni.* Prag, CSLH.

Pavliš, Z. (1995): *Školeni trenérů ledniho hokeje. Vybrané obecné obory.* Prag, CSLH.

Stenlund, K. Vern. (1996): *Hockey drills for puck control.* Illinois, Human Kinetics.

PHOTO & ILLUSTRATION CREDITS

Cover design: Jens Vogelsang
Cover photo: Asa Fotoagentur
Internal Photos: Asa Fotoagentur
Graphics: Jens Vogelsang
Diagrams: Jana Tvrznikova